MOTIVATING TODAY'S WORK FORCE

MOTIVATING TODAY'S WORK FORCE
When the carrot can't always be cash

Lin Grensing

Self-Counsel Press
(a division of)
International Self-Counsel Press Ltd.
Canada U.S.A.

Printed in Canada
First Self-Counsel edition: April, 1991

Canadian Cataloguing in Publication Data
    Grensing, Lin, 1959–
    Motivating today's work force
    (Self-counsel business series)
    ISBN 0-88908-955-8
    1. Employee motivation. I. Title. II. Series.
    HF5549.5.M63G73 1991 658.3'14 C91-091014-6

Cover photo by Brian Leng/Image Finders, Vancouver

Self-Counsel Press
(a division of)
International Self-Counsel Press Ltd.
Head and Editorial Office
1481 Charlotte Road
North Vancouver, British Columbia V7J 1H1

U.S. Address
1704 N. State Street
Bellingham, Washington 98225

CONTENTS

LIST OF SAMPLES

LIST OF WORKSHEETS

INTRODUCTION
MOTIVATING TODAY'S WORK FORCE

Businesses in the United States and Canada are experiencing a growing concern for the level of productivity of their workers. Statistics have shown that not only is productivity slowly decreasing, but the available qualified work force is shrinking as well. No longer can employers feel that, when a good employee leaves the company, they'll "find someone else just as good." Now, more than ever, employers feel the need to hang on to their current employees.

But a new generation of employees is entering the labor market, a group that differs in many respects from the baby boomer generation that preceded it. These workers, according to a recent *Time* magazine article, want to "avoid risk, pain and rapid change" and are "considered overly sensitive at best and lazy at worst." If the employees of this new generation are to commit themselves to an employer and do their best work, they must be carefully cared for. They must be nurtured.

They must be motivated.

In a survey by Grotta, Glassman & Hoffman cited in *US News & World Report*, 69% of company managers said that the thing that annoys them most about their employees is lack of motivation. These managers are right to be concerned about unmotivated employees, but what they need to realize is that motivated employees are the product of good management — and that is *their* responsibility.

Business owners and managers wonder, "Are we making the best use of our human resources?" "Are we keeping the people who work for us happy, motivated, and loyal?" "How can we continue to (or begin to) motivate our current work force, given that we're in a slump, in the red, or in a pinch?" "How can we motivate our employees so they will help our company grow and how can we accomplish this without adding to the already high costs of our operations?"

The good news is that money is *not* the only or even the most important motivator. In a survey conducted by human resources consultants Wick & Co., a group of employees of Fortune 500 companies were asked to name the most likely reason they'd leave their jobs. Fewer than 10% cited money as a factor. The new generation of employees is much less concerned with money than were their predecessors and tend to scoff at the crass materialism of the past.

Several years ago, I worked for a governmental agency where I was well-paid but underutilized. I left that position to take a position with a private company at a substantially lower salary. My new position proved to be challenging, exciting…and motivating.

Since that time, I have been a strong advocate of nonmonetary incentives — the little things that go a long way to boost employee morale and strengthen employee loyalty.

This book will show business owners and managers how to —

(a) understand what motivates their employees,

(b) apply widely accepted motivational theories to their business,

(c) develop nonmonetary incentives that will help their employees and their company grow,

(d) apply nonmonetary incentives consistently and fairly, and

(e) save the company money and boost profits by motivating employees for improved productivity.

This book is a tribute to the thousands of employers who already recognize the importance of "nonmonetaries." It's also a gentle push to the thousands of employers who don't.

From a pat on the back to the establishment of a management-by-objectives program, *Motivating Today's Work Force* explores the many nonmonetary options available to employers of the nineties.

PART I
LAYING THE GROUNDWORK

When someone suggests that you use "nonmonetary" incentives to motivate your employees, are you tempted to say, "There's no such thing as a free lunch"? Do you mentally add up the cost of these "nonmonetary" incentives? Do you seriously question the effectiveness of such things as a "pat on the back" or "employee of the month" awards?In short, do you doubt that nonmonetary incentives can get the people you pay for a day's work to give you what you're paying for?

Well, you're not alone.

However, it may surprise you to know that many companies find nonmonetary incentives to be both effective and economical.

Let's deal with your first concern right away. You're right. These incentives may be nonmonetary to your employees but they still cost you money, whether you're sponsoring an employee softball team or giving your "employee of the month" an afternoon off. *Somebody* has to pay for these incentives and that somebody is going to be you.

Your second question is whether these incentives are effective. Many employers believe they are. Of course, if an employee is not being paid "enough," no non-monetary reward will cure a productivity problem. What's "enough"? That depends. And while this is not a book on compensation plans, it is important to deal briefly with this issue. "Enough," for most people, is what they see as fair — in the context of the company and in the context of the employment community. An employee wants assurance that his or her level of pay is commensurate with that of other employees performing comparable work with comparable experience

1

who have been with the company for a comparable period of time. Further, they want to know that their level of pay is comparable to that of their peers performing comparable jobs at other companies in the area. If, as a business owner or manager, you're confident that you're fulfilling these two basic requirements of providing a fair salary, your next task (the one dealt with in this book) is encouraging employees to higher levels of achievement. That's where motivation comes into play.

Robert Glegg, president of Glegg Water Conditioning Inc. in Guelph, Ontario, agrees that fair wages are just the beginning. In the May, 1990, issue of *Canadian Business*, where his firm was listed as one of Canada's best-managed private companies, Glegg is quoted as saying "Paying someone a lot is never a positive on its own. It merely removes a possible negative."

Let's look at an example to illustrate why money isn't always the most important motivator — why, in many cases, it will absolutely *not* cause a worker to increase his or her productivity.

Deb has been working at XYZ company for eight years. She's received several very generous raises and currently makes what she considers to be an extremely fair salary. But she's not really happy in her job and her performance is declining. An increase in pay won't make her happy. It won't make her increase her productivity. What will? As we'll see, there are a number of motivators that *will* improve performance, from simple forms of recognition like certificates of achievement, to added responsibility, educational benefits, and flexible work schedules.

1
NONMONETARY INCENTIVES AND MOTIVATIONAL THEORY

Motivation is a hard term to define. It's even harder to identify it when selecting employees and to foster it when developing employees. Still, as a manager, you can usually recognize motivation when you see it.

You recognize motivation in the line worker who not only produces more widgets in a day than any other worker, but also develops new and better ways of producing widgets and shares these techniques with fellow employees.

You recognize motivation in the sales clerk who volunteers to work extra hours during busy seasonal sales.

Motivation is evident in the employee who works harder, more effectively, and with more enthusiasm than the average employee.

Motivation is drive. It's ambition. And it's a behavior that's missing in many workers. Its absence is directly related to the way many managers manage.

a. WHAT THE THEORISTS TELL US

Business theorists have long speculated on how workers are encouraged to do more in less time and be happy about doing it.

1. Maintainers vs. motivators

In the 1950s, industrial psychologist Frederick Herzberg found that certain job factors caused worker dissatisfaction and poor performance when they fell below a certain level.

Yet, these same factors failed to *increase* job performance once they reached an optimum level. He labeled these factors *maintainers* because they maintain a certain level of productivity.

Salary, job security, company policies, and administration are all classified as maintainers. Once these factors reach an optimum level, merely providing more of them will not produce an increase in productivity.

Herzberg also identified several sources of job satisfaction that he called *motivators*. These include achievement, recognition for achievement, the work itself, responsibility, and advancement. Motivators make employees work harder. The more motivators there are, the harder an employee will work.

Maintainers merely maintain a behavior. While they must be present for a positive behavior to continue, increasing them will not necessarily result in an increase in performance. *Decreasing* a maintainer, though, will almost certainly result in a decrease in work performance.

2. The Hierarchy of Needs

Another early theorist was Abraham Maslow, a psychologist who developed what he called a "need hierarchy." He classified five levels of needs ranging from the concrete to the intangible. These needs are: physiological comfort, safety, social fulfillment, satisfaction of the ego, and self-actualization.

All are, for the most part, inter-related. For instance, while we strive to earn a good wage, we are also concerned with attaining job stability, getting along with coworkers, being admired, and enjoying the work we do.

As we go through the series of needs, however, they become harder and harder to satisfy. It is the job of the company, the manager, or "the boss" to satisfy these higher level needs.

The average employee is 85% satisfied in terms of physiological needs, 70% in terms of safety needs, 50% in terms of social needs, 40% in terms of ego needs — but only 10% in terms of self-actualization needs. Obviously, the supervisor or manager would be wise to spend the most time satisfying the needs at the upper end of the hierarchy — social fulfillment, satisfaction of the ego, and self-actualization.

Which brings us to Theories X and Y.

3. Theories X and Y

Strongly influenced by Maslow and his need hierarchy, Douglas McGregor applied this hierarchy to the organizational structure. In the 1960s, he came up with two opposing theories which he called Theory X and Theory Y.

Theory X management stresses that human beings are lazy and avoid work.They need to receive direction and are motivated through the fear of punishment. In addition, Theory X proposes that the average employee tries to avoid responsibility and wants job security above all else.

Theory Y management states that people will use both self-control and self-direction.This theory suggests that the average employee learns not only to accept but to seek responsibility.

Theory X organizations have a hierarchical structure and control employee behavior. Employees are treated as if they—

(a) are lazy and anxious to avoid work whenever possible,

(b) need control and direction in order to perform well,

(c) have relatively little ambition, and

(d) avoid responsibility whenever possible.

Theory Y organizations, on the other hand, are characterized by integration. According to McGregor, integration involves "the creation of conditions such that the members of the organization can achieve their goals best by directing their efforts toward the success of the enterprise." Employees are treated as if they—

(a) enjoy physical and mental effort,

(b) direct themselves to meet objectives,

(c) relate achievement with certain rewards, and

(d) use a high degree of imagination, ingenuity, and creativity.

4. Theory Z

Theory Z is a more recent theory advanced by William Ouchi.

The secret to Japanese success, according to Ouchi, is not technology but a special way of managing people. This management style involves a strong company philosophy, a distinct corporate culture, long-range staff development, and consensus decision making. The result is lower turnover, increased job commitment, and much higher productivity.

A major aspect of Theory Z is trust. Organizations spend a lot of time developing the interpersonal skills needed to make effective group decisions. When a group makes decisions, group members are asked to place their fate in the hands of others. Each person has responsibility for some individual objectives set by the group. Team performance is critical to the accomplishment of objectives.

Ouchi has said:

> Perhaps the single most notable characteristic among those who have succeeded at going from A to Z has been an almost palpable character of integrity. By integrity I do not mean preaching morality to others; I mean an

integrated response to problems, an integrated and consistent response to customers and employees, to superiors and subordinates, to problems in finance and in manufacturing. A person of integrity treats secretaries. and executives with equal respect and approaches subordinates with the same understanding and values that characterize his family relationships. A person with integrity can be counted upon to behave consistently even as organizational conditions change. Such a person can be trusted and can provide that key human capital from which others can draw in the process of change.

b. APPLYING THE THEORIES

Theories and classification systems are a good starting point for employers and managers looking for ways to improve employee performance, morale, and productivity. For real results, however, you need more than theory. You need a step-by-step, day-by-day, practical approach to motivating your employees so they will help your company run smoothly and profitably. How you motivate your employees without adding to the already high costs of your operations is the challenge that today's manager faces. To deal with this challenge, more and more managers are turning to nonmonetary incentives for employee motivation.

Yes, the managers who cynically remark "There's no such thing as a free lunch" are right.Of course it's going to cost money to give an outstanding employee a day off. It is going to cost money to have a spur-of-the-moment party on a Friday afternoon. But unmotivated employees are going to cost a lot more in the long run.

2
HOW TO AVOID THE MOTIVATIONAL FALLACIES

"Motivation" has become something of a buzzword these days. It is also surrounded by many myths and misconceptions. Before going any further, let's try to clear up some of these myths.

a. FALLACY #1 — MONEY IS AN EFFECTIVE MOTIVATOR

The idea that money is an effective motivator is perhaps the most common motivational myth. In fact, this book is based on the belief that money can *not* be an effective motivator *once an optimum level of pay is reached.*

Let's look at an example.

John Smith has been hired, at minimum wage, to work for Marshall Manufacturing as a widget counter. At first, John is glad to have a job. Later, his performance declines. Once he has mastered the simple task of counting widgets, he begins to become dissatisfied with his salary. He's paid substantially less than widget counters at other companies in the area.

Mr. Kingpin, John's supervisor, senses John's dissatisfaction and guesses that he's unhappy with his pay. Because John is a good worker and important to Marshall Manufacturing, Mr. Kingpin gives him a substantial increase in pay. John's performance increases initially, but widget counting no longer provides a challenge. Although he's now satisfied with his pay, he doesn't feel like going to work in the morning. John's performance again declines, he is frequently absent from work, and he is looking for another job.

John's level of pay has reached an optimum level and more money will not be a motivator for him. No matter how much more he's paid, he will not become more satisfied or productive.

After looking at the John Smith example, you'll probably concede that, at best, money is a good "sweetener." While it's a necessary aspect of any job, it's not enough to keep performance at a high level in the absence of other things — things like recognition, involvement, and good communication. While a cake has to have sugar to make it taste good, it won't be a cake unless all the other ingredients are there. In the same way, in any job, money may make a position seem very attractive, but in the absence of other nonmonetary aspects of a job, it won't be enough to keep an employee happy.

As we saw in chapter 1, Frederick Herzberg determined that some factors in a work situation had the power to make people feel dissatisfied. These "maintainers" resulted in poor performance if they fell below a certain level, but failed to increase job performance once they reached an optimum level. Money must, at best, be classified as one of these "maintainers."

The effectiveness of money as a motivator is also lessened by the common attitude, "I'll work until I have enough money to pay the bills, but then I'll opt for leisure time."

While many people argue that money is an effective motivator, they have a hard time explaining the fact that survey after survey reveals increasing discontent even though today's workers are better paid and have more benefits than at any other time in history.

In *The Gold Collar Worker* (Addison-Wesley, 1985), Robert E. Kelley writes, "Money, of course, isn't everything to workers....Gold collar workers also will demand regular and meaningful nonmonetary rewards. Before sharing their knowledge with an employer, they require a work environment characterized by mutual trust in which they can enjoy the psychological rewards they feel they deserve. In essence, organizations will maintain emotional bank accounts with their employees. If they make periodic deposits, employees will cooperate and perform. If the balance dwindles or is overdrawn, gold-collar account holders, sooner or later, will do their banking elsewhere."

Yes, you'll have to pay your workers, and pay them fairly, if you want a good job done. After a certain point, though — and this point will vary with each employee — money will no longer serve as an effective motivator. It is at this point that you'll need to turn to nonmonetary incentives.

b. FALLACY #2 — MOTIVATION = PRODUCTIVITY

George S. Odiorne, one of the early members of the Management by Objectives (MBO) movement, defines *motivation* as a hidden force that causes us to take an action. Motivation can't be directly observed; it must be inferred from behavior. Because motivation is a hidden force, it is very difficult to quantify.

One way to attempt to quantify motivation is by looking at the measurable results of the behavior caused by motivation: *productivity*. Productivity is a measure of the action taken as a result of motivation. At the other end of this chain of cause and effect are the *motivators*, those things that create motivation and start the chain going. This is how the sequence goes:

Motivators —(create)→ Motivation —(causes)→ Behavior —(effects)→ Productivity

10

Let's look at an example.

Constance is the manager of a group of 10 widget crunchers. They work the hours of 11:00 p.m. to 7:00 a.m. five days a week. They must occasionally work an extra shift on Saturdays. The job is routine and simplistic. Each widget cruncher was hired at the same time and each is paid the same hourly rate of pay. Widget production is at an all-time low of 250 widgets crunched per hour — 25 widgets per employee.

Upper management is shocked and baffled. What's going on? What's happened to productivity in the Crunch Department? Constance is called in and asked to increase production by *at least* 10% during the next month. If she can't do it, she must begin looking for employment elsewhere.

With this in mind, Constance does several things:

(a) She calls a meeting of the 10 crunchers in her department and chastises them for their slow work. She lets them know that if she goes some of them may also go.

(b) She asks for their assistance in coming up with ideas on increasing production.

(c) She singles out two of the widget crunchers to supervise four other widget crunchers.

(d) She decides to hold weekly production meetings to monitor progress and "trouble-shoot."

(e) She sets up another shift to allow for more scheduling flexibility.

(f) She spends a lot more time out "on the floor" with the crunchers. She helps them over trouble spots and congratulates them when they do something particularly well.

At the end of a month, productivity has increased 25%! Top management is ecstatic. Constance is vindicated. The crunchers are relieved.

11

What happened here?

(a) Constance was motivated by the threat to her job security (a motivator — yes, even negative incentives can be motivating).

(b) The crunchers were motivated through a series of events that included a threat to *their* job security, employee involvement, recognition, flex-time, and participation (motivators).

(c) Constance and her crunching team changed their behavior.

(d) Management realized its goal of 10% increase in production (and then some). Productivity was increased.

There are a couple of problems, however. First, neither Constance nor top management will be able to pinpoint what caused this increase in production. It's difficult to quantify the impact of the various approaches used.

Second, chances are that with the increase in productivity, Constance will relax some of her newly devised procedures and, slowly, productivity will drop.

There are other reasons that motivation is a hard issue to deal with:

- Motivation is a very personal thing. The force that drives one employee to work harder may have no impact on another employee. The same force may even decrease the performance of some employees.

- The goals of the employee may not be the goals of the company. In the above example a few of the crunchers may not have cared whether productivity increased. In fact, they may have looked forward to the possibility of being laid off and the opportunity to collect unemployment.

- Some employees can be very highly motivated and still be unproductive. There may be other problems that are hindering performance — problems such as ability, knowledge, and equipment.

Remember — *motivation* cannot be directly measured, quantified, or labeled. It is a drive. *Productivity* can be measured in terms of an increase or decrease in a specific task. The manager's job, then, is to determine those variables that *will* produce motivation which, in turn, increases productivity.

c. FALLACY #3 — MANAGERS CAN MOTIVATE

Nobody can *cause* a smoker to stop smoking, or an alcoholic to stop drinking, or a gambler to stop gambling. No manager can *cause* an employee to be motivated. But, a manager can provide the *means* for motivation to take place.

An employee will be motivated when he or she has an unmet need — an *individual* need. When this need exists, employees will take steps on their own to satisfy the need.

As a manager, though, you are in a position to —

(a) recognize an unmet need,

(b) determine and present to the employee a means (or various means) to satisfy the need, and

(c) monitor the results.

Remember the old carrot and the stick story? If the horse hadn't wanted the carrot (need), *no* carrot, regardless of how succulent, could cause it to move forward. In this proverb, however, the horse apparently had a fondness for carrots. Still, the farmer did not motivate the horse. The farmer simply provided a means by which the horse could satisfy a need.

That's what you must do with your employees.

13

d. FALLACY #4 — HAPPY EMPLOYEES ARE PRODUCTIVE EMPLOYEES

Happy employees are happy employees. That's it. If all you want is happy employees, then this isn't such a bad thing. However, if you're looking for productivity, you need to look a little further.

Another problem with this myth is that, if you believe it, you may not spot employees who are quietly motivated.

The bottom line? Callous as it may seem, you're really not concerned with motivation as a drive, but with the expression of that drive — productivity. You're looking for output. Unfortunately, a smile just doesn't do it.

e. FALLACY #5 — MOTIVATORS ARE UNIVERSAL

Motivators are *not* universal. One employee may be delighted that you care enough to remember his birthday and improve his output 200% while another employee may sneer when she's awarded the Employee of the Year Award and may show no improvement in productivity.

Some employees simply want to do their jobs. They work at a fair but even pace. They are neither satisfied nor dissatisfied. They are not upwardly mobile.

Some employees are like small children. They need to be constantly prodded. Their managers are always trying to think of creative ways to provide incentives and boost productivity.

Some employees are easily motivated. They respond to almost *any* change in their environment — positive or negative.

Some employees are powerhouses of productivity. They are self-motivators. Their environment may seem free of any motivator yet they consistently perform at or beyond their limit.

The point is, every employee is different. Therefore every employee will need to have different incentives applied to achieve the same end — productivity.

f. FALLACY #6 — DISINCENTIVES CAN BE USED TO AID IN MOTIVATION

If you can't get an employee to do the job, you can always resort to some form of punishment to "teach a lesson," right? Well, you can, but behavioral psychologists have demonstrated for years that negative reinforcement is less effective as a means of changing behavior than positive reinforcement.

Certainly there are times when disciplinary action is necessary. Use caution, however, is applying discipline in the hope that you will be able to "whip" your employees into shape.

g. FALLACY #7 — A MANAGER DOESN'T HAVE TO BE PERSONALLY MOTIVATED TO HAVE A MOTIVATED STAFF

Joan is the manager of a five-person staff. For the past six months her attitude has markedly declined. She rarely works full days, spends her time on the job in long discussions with coworkers, and has begun to shirk extra responsibility whenever possible.

When her manager calls her in to talk about the effect of her attitude on her staff she's shocked: "How can the way I feel have anything to do with them? They've got great jobs. I can't believe you don't feel they're motivated."

The fact of the matter is, they're probably not feeling very motivated. It's disheartening to work for a leader who shows no enthusiasm or excitement for the job being done.

If, as a manager, you're not feeling very motivated (for whatever reasons) take care not to let it show to your staff. You'll only be compounding your problems.

h. FALLACY #8 — IF MY EMPLOYEES ARE MOTIVATED, I'LL BE ABLE TO SEE IT

Almost the reverse of #4, this fallacy is also a common misconception in management ranks. Motivation can't be measured by "smile-o-meter." Some employees are naturally stoic. Their seemingly lackluster demeanor is not necessarily a reflection of lack of motivation.

Certainly, as a manager, you need to be on the lookout for overt signs of employee behavior problems. However, what you're typically looking for is a change in some baseline behavior. If a normally vivacious, energetic employee is suddenly dragging around the office looking glum, you probably can assume that his or her motivation level is declining.

However, if you've just hired a new employee who exhibits the same characteristics, don't jump to conclusions. The behavior may simply be a reflection of that individual's personality.

i. FALLACY #9 — MIDDLE MANAGEMENT IS RESPONSIBLE FOR MAINTAINING A MOTIVATED STAFF

Motivation follows the "trickle-down" rule. If the middle manager isn't motivated, it's going to be almost impossible for that manager to motivate his or her staff. Even if the middle manager *is* motivated and knows how to motivate others, a lackluster upper management team can stifle any of the positive effects the middle manager has on the staff.

If your company suffers from a disheartened upper management team, perhaps you need to look upward for the root of your employees' motivation problems.

j. FALLACY #10 — IF THREE OUT OF YOUR FOUR EMPLOYEES ARE MOTIVATED, YOU REALLY HAVE NOTHING TO WORRY ABOUT

Remember "one bad apple can spoil the whole bushel." This is true of employees as well. If just one person in your department has a motivation problem, that problem can easily spread to others on the staff.

How to avoid this?

- Try to intercede in any interdepartmental negative discussions that take place — turn the negatives into positives

- Make an extra effort to provide extra incentives to the entire staff

- Hold frequent group meetings where you can head off many of the negative "vibes" that the unhappy employee is exuding

Are these the only fallacies? Certainly not. There are as many fallacies circulating about employee motivation as there are employees who are not motivated. Some of the following statements may be familiar to you:

"Why should I worry about motivation? They're doing the job, aren't they?"

"She should be happy, she has a job."

"Motivation is all theory. It doesn't have any practical application in the workplace."

"Nobody's irreplaceable."

You've probably heard some of the above fallacies from coworkers, fellow businesspeople, friends, and relatives. You may have even expressed some of them yourself. Don't feel bad. The above myths are listed because they're so common. If you're one of the people who has believed one or more in the past, you're not alone. But, if you're one of the people who is going to read on and develop new ways to respond to "North America's productivity challenge" you're already a step ahead of some of your competitors.

3
HOW TO DETERMINE WHAT MOTIVATES EMPLOYEES

a. MOTIVATORS FOR THE 1990s

No two people are the same. No two of your employees are the same. Consequently, no single motivator is going to work with all of your employees. To motivate effectively with nonmonetary incentives you need to know more than what the motivators are. You need to know what motivators will work with *your* people — each one of them.

The needs and values of 1990s workers are very different from the needs and values of 1950s workers. Today's workers are better educated, less interested in following orders, more loyal to themselves than to the company, and more concerned about meeting their own needs.

The 1990s employee —

(a) wants meaningful work,

(b) spends a lot of time in leisure activities,

(c) is both overconfident and self-doubting,

(d) has a strong need for feedback and recognition, and

(e) is impatient and unwilling to wait long for payback on effort.The current generation of workers can be very difficult to motivate. According to the Bureau of Labor Statistics, more than 71,000,000 people between the ages of 25 and 45 will begin working by the year 1995. At the same time the number of management jobs will fall sharply. In 1980, there were approximately three candidates for every two management jobs. In 1995, this ratio will increase to 5:1. All this competition for jobs means that more of today's workers will have to come to terms with being "stuck" in the same job without much hope for changing employment or even promotion.

What happens when an employee works at the same job, year after year, with no chance for promotion? She or he becomes dissatisfied and, eventually, non-productive. To maintain job satisfaction under these circumstances, employers must come up with creative ideas for employee motivation. To do this, they must first determine what motivates their employees.

b. WHAT EMPLOYEES WANT

Many employers assume they know what their workers want and believe they are providing it. For example, they may point to good wage and benefit packages as proof that they are doing well by their employees. But sometimes when we think we know what motivates our workforce we may be wrong.

A 1969 study by the Research Center of the University of Michigan looked at the attitudes of 1533 workers at different occupational levels. *All* ranked interesting work and the authority to get the job done far ahead of good pay and job security. These same findings were confirmed in 1973 and 1978 studies.

In 1984, 327 school principals from Alberta were asked to complete a questionnaire assessing their job satisfaction. Eight satisfaction factors were identified through factor analysis and three were determined to contribute the most to overall job satisfaction: responsibility and autonomy, principal-teacher work involvement, and liaison at the district level.

20

Salary and benefits did not contribute significantly to the overall job satisfaction of those taking the survey.

Do you really know what your employees want? To determine just how much your perception of what your employees want differs from what they really want, complete Worksheet #1 and ask your employees to complete it also. The differences in the way you rank different aspects of employment may surprise you.

WORKSHEET #1
MOTIVATORS

Rank from 1 to 10 (10 being the least wanted) what you think your employees want from their jobs. Circulate the list to your employees, asking them to rank the order of importance from their perspective.

	Your Rank	Employee Rank
Help with personal problems	_____	_____
Interesting work	_____	_____
High wages	_____	_____
Job security	_____	_____
Personal loyalty of supervisor	_____	_____
Tactful discipline	_____	_____
Full appreciation of work done	_____	_____
Feeling of belonging	_____	_____
Good working conditions	_____	_____
Promotion in the company	_____	_____

A 30-year study conducted by the Minnesota Gas Company indicated that the most powerful incentives for employees, in order of importance, were the following:

(a) promotion

(b) enjoyable and interesting work

(c) a company they are proud of

(d) job security

(e) a big salary

(f) a fair and considerate supervisor

(g) pleasant coworkers

(h) benefits such as health care, vacation, sick pay, and pension

(i) clean and comfortable work areas

(j) "good" hours of work

So don't assume you know what your employees want. You may be in for a shock when you find out what they *really* want.

c. HOW TO FIND OUT WHAT YOUR EMPLOYEES WANT

How can you determine what motivates your employees?

(a) Ask them. Go to each of your employees and ask them what things they like most (and least) about their jobs. Ask them specifically, "What are some of the things that the company does to increase your self-esteem?" "What are some of the things that the company does to decrease your self-esteem." Their answers will give you the starting point you need to develop some effective ways of motivating them.

(b) Find out what your employees do in their spare time — both at work and at home. Observe them during

22

break periods and lunch hours. Do they spend their time relaxing? Socializing? Reading? Working?

(c) Take into consideration past experiences. To what has the employee responded favorably in the past? What type of projects or assignments really create a high level of productivity? What types of assignments create apathy?

It's a mistake to transfer your own likes, dislikes, and desires to employees. To motivate your employees, you need to tailor incentives to the employees' individual needs.

One way of doing this is to use a survey. Dick Berry, an associate professor of management and administrator of Management Institute's marketing management program, has developed a survey instrument called Motiquiz III, shown here as Worksheet #2. This survey contains 45 statements describing different situations. Each statement in the Motiquiz represents one of the five levels in Maslow's Hierarchy of Needs. Ask your employees to identify the statements that describe conditions that would make them do their best work.

Berry has used Motiquiz with several thousand people from different types of work environments. He has found that over three-quarters selected the statement "Being trusted to do my job the way it should be done."

The simplest way to find out what motivates your employees is to talk to them. Another way is to observe them. Knowing the interests of your employees when they are away from work is as helpful as knowing their interests on the job. It's not just nice to express interest in your employees — it's vital to effective nonmonetary management.

MOTIQUIZ

An exercise to determine motivational needs

To perform the exercise, read through the following statements. Check those that are **most important in motivating you to do your best work.** Select the *ten* most important statements. See scoring guide at bottom after you've made the selections.

629   Job security because of seniority or employment contract arrangements

847   Being trusted to do my job the way I think it should be done

333   Participating in work group conversations

311   Having adequate shelter to protect from the elements

836   Having a job which allows me time with my family

151   Having an opportunity for personal growth

937   Socializing with my friends

743   Being considered for an advancement opportunity

431   Working with other people

819   Having children

458   Doing something meaningful with my life

757   Being in a position to contribute new ideas

828   Having an associate that looks out for my interests

215 Not having to do exhausting work or do extra work at home

421 Having steady work

654 Being able to express my full potential

327 Knowing that I will always have a job

912 Having rest breaks with nourishment available

924 Having a healthful working environment

548 Being given a new interesting job

256 Having the opportunity for self-improvement

722 Having protection from physical harm

352 Being able to learn and grow in my work

735 Including other people in what I do

949 Being selected for an exclusive award

234 Being involved with work associates in social and recreational activities

616 Being sexually satisfied

146 Having a responsible person tell me when I've done a good job

539 Having an active part in work-related social activities

341 Knowing that other people respect me and my work

132 Acceptance as a work group member

225 Having insurance or other protective benefits

444	Having others recognize the importance of my job
853	Having a new and exciting job challenge
113	Having enough food to eat each day
245	Not having to be responsible to other people
517	Having personal comfort in my working environment
126	Knowing what is expected of me in my work
559	Having the opportunity to express myself fully and creatively
718	Having good air to breathe
638	Working with persons I want to associate with
642	Having a position of authority
523	A guaranteed income
955	The personal satisfaction of a job well done
414	Assurance that I will have adequate clothing to protect from the elements

Scoring Instructions for Motiquiz

To determine results: The statements are divided into five categories intended to represent the five levels in Maslow's Hierarchy of Needs. The second digit in each statement number indicates the category. These categories are:

1 — Physiological

2 — Safety/security

3 — Love/belonging

4 — Self-esteem

5 — Self-actualization

The employee's motivational needs are *suggested* by the number of selections in each category. For example, if he or she had one 1, two 2s, one 3, four 4s, and two 5s, the percentages would be:

Physiological — 10%

Safety/security — 20%

Love/belonging — 10%

Self-esteem — 40%

Self-actualization — 20%

d. HOW TO USE INCENTIVES

The following examples of employees with specific needs show how you can recognize these needs and use nonmonetary incentives to improve performance.

Harry is a 36-year-old assembly-line worker in a tire manufacturing plant. He is married, has two children, and owns his home in an upper middle-class neighborhood. After work, he participates in intramural sports programs and is a member of several local civic groups. Harry is a good worker. However, he is starting to complain about the long hours, the heat in the summer, and the short breaks.

As Harry's supervisor, you note his discontent. You know Harry receives a generous salary. You also know that Harry is not career oriented. He's at the physiological stage of the hierarchy — satisfying his basic needs, nothing more. You decide to —

- let Harry have the option of working a shorter week,

- improve some of the working conditions in the plant,

- allow longer rest periods, and

- suggest that lunch breaks be taken outside the plant for a change of pace.

There are many employees like Harry who are trying only to satisfy physiological needs. Many employees are not interested in such things as participation in policy-making or promotion.

Joan is in a middle-management position at a small insurance company. For two years she has reported to a Mr. Harris Johnson, a man she gets along with well. Last month, Mr. Johnson transferred suddenly to a different department, leaving the position above her vacant. Joan, always a very dependable woman, has begun to come in late. She often misses work for "unexplainable" illnesses. She fails to complete various assignments. The owner of the company is

28

upset. She is seriously questioning Joan's ability to continue in her position.

By using the hierarchy of needs to identify employee motivation, you would know that Joan is trying to satisfy her security needs. When Mr. Johnson unexpectedly changed positions, Joan was confused about her own position with the company. Would she be offered a promotion? Would she be expected to accept? Would the new manager like her work? Would she be terminated? These and many other questions were running through her mind daily as her work came undone and her spirits fell.

Communication and involvement are the most important tools for motivating employees who are seeking security. The biggest threats to these employees are poor communication, lack of clear policy, poor management, favoritism or discrimination, and automation. Arbitrary action or unexplained changes can be very threatening.

In this case, the owner of the insurance company called Joan in to ask her about her recent change of behavior. After a long talk, the owner assured Joan that much consideration would go into hiring a new manager. The new manager would not have the authority to re-staff the department. Joan also learned that she would not be expected to fill the position.

Tim had worked as a janitor at Caledonia High School for six months and still didn't feel that he belonged. Few people talked to him during the day and those that did, wanted something. "Empty the trash in room 140." "Clean up the spilled milk in the cafeteria." "Do this." "Do that."

Tim's supervisor recognized the problem almost immediately, but didn't know how to correct it. You can't *make* people like somebody and Tim just wasn't popular. The supervisor really didn't know what to do.

For people attempting to satisfy the social needs of work life, like Tim, belonging is very important. Unfriendly associates and management or office cliques can kill productivity when social needs aren't met.

Tim's supervisor is right, you can't make people like a fellow employee. What you *can* do is set an example by showing that *you* like and respect the unpopular employee. Others may take your lead.

Sondra has worked at XYZ Manufacturing as a billing clerk for 15 years. She is recognized both for her careful attention to detail and her exceptionally high level of productivity — known so well, in fact, that her performance is taken for granted. She hears praise so infrequently that the slightest criticism makes her "fly off the handle." She's becoming increasingly defensive and her manager wants to know why.

When an employee gets to a high level of need achievement like the ego level, need satisfaction becomes more difficult. Sondra's manager can, however, try one or more of the following:

- Careful use of rewards and recognition

- Job enlargement or expansion of duties

- Training and development — perhaps for a management position

- More frequent and informal performance appraisals

One of the worst things a manager can do is fail to provide adequate praise and reinforcement.

Janine, an advertising manager, sincerely enjoyed her work. She even enjoyed the daily aggravations that seemed to increase all the time. She was becoming more and more vocal, however, about top management policies and was beginning to be considered a troublemaker.

At the highest level of Maslow's hierarchy of needs, the self-actualization level, you'll find your most promising employees. These are your star players. They may also be your troublemakers.

For people like Janine you need to have progressive policies and progressive business planning. You also need to create and maintain opportunities for self-expression and you need to learn to tolerate individualism. You *don't* want to create inflexible policies or squelch ideas — even the kind you may initially view as troublesome.

e. CONCLUSION

The above examples are not intended to suggest that Maslow's hierarchy is the only measure of employee motives that you should use. It is simply a guideline that can prove very helpful for determining the best ways to motivate employees.

What happens if you don't pay attention to your employees' wants and needs? Well, low productivity is one thing. High turnover is another. You don't want either, so you should begin paying attention today.

PART II
GIVING THEM WHAT THEY WANT

What are the most common laments heard from today's employees?

- "I just don't know what my boss expects from me."

- "I thought I was doing a good job — then all of a sudden wham!"

- "If I'm doing something wrong, I want to know what it is."

- "If I'm doing something right, I expect some positive feedback."

- "All I ever hear is what I'm doing *wrong*."

- "Nobody recognizes the things I do."

"You can lead a horse to water, but you can't make him drink." With a bit of variation, this old saying can just as easily apply to your employees. "You can lead an employee to the typewriter (or drill press, or computer terminal, or boardroom) but you can't make him or her work."

Why do people work? There are many different answers and, chances are, you'll never get the same one twice. Unfortunately, the expectations that people bring to their jobs rarely equal the ability of the job to meet these expectations.

Toni is 18 and saving money for college. Her motivation for working is strictly monetary and she expects little from her job as a shipping clerk.

Kevin, at 35, has worked hard to achieve his position as vice-president of marketing for a large firm. The aspect of his position that gives him the most enjoyment is his ability to network with fellow executives, to speak at various conventions, and to build a name for himself in his field of expertise. Kevin's motivation for working is prestige.

Kari has a job as secretary with a new company where the other 15 employees are all in her age range — mid- to late twenties. She plays on the company softball team, helps to organize various employee get-togethers, and spends most of her off-duty hours socializing with coworkers. The motivating factor for Kari is socialization.

As you've probably noticed, the reasons people give for working closely parallel Maslow's hierarchy of needs. But don't be misled into thinking that these reasons are limited to the five aspects of this hierarchy. The number of reasons that employees have for working can be as varied as the number of companies there are to work for!

Your job as a manager is further complicated because, as we've already seen, there is a vast difference between what will motivate one person and what will motivate another. One employee may become very productive after being praised for a job well done, while another may show no change.

Even negative recognition (criticism) can have an impact on performance. Again, the exact impact will vary with the individual. While criticism may cause one employee to do a better job it may cause another employee's performance to drop.

Of course, even positive recognition can cause negative reactions. And sometimes things that don't even seem like recognition can have a dramatic impact on performance.

The Hawthorne Experiment is a good example of this. The experiment was conducted during a five-year period from 1927 to 1932. Five women were placed in a room where their work was carefully controlled, their output was measured, and they were closely observed. At intervals, changes were made in their working conditions and the effects of these changes were monitored.

The outcome was an increase in productivity each time something in the environment was changed. It was more than just these changes causing the upswing in productivity, however. Some other factors were at work:

- Supervision was minimal

- The women were allowed to participate in decision-making

- They were frequently called in and asked questions about their opinions, their fears, and their well-being

They were recognized. Finally, someone noticed they were there. Noticed so much, in fact, that virtually every move they made was monitored and every concern or problem they had was listened to intently and sincerely.

The Hawthorne Experiment was one of the first indications that something other than money has an impact on employee output.

What do your employees really want and how can you give it to them? Let's take a look.

4
GOAL SETTING

The guiding principle in goal setting is this: if you want them to "do as you say," make sure you tell them what you want and make sure you say it clearly.

At Pacific Gas and Electric Co., each manager is required to clearly communicate to every one of his or her employees —

(a) the changes occurring in the business,

(b) the nature of the two markets served,

(c) the need to become a more market-driven company, and

(d) how corporate goals set objectives for success as a market-driven company. According to chairman of the board and CEO Richard A. Clarke, "to achieve superior results from our employees, we must make certain they know what's expected of them and why. Each manager must clearly communicate this to every one of his or her people."

Did you ever ask an employee why they didn't do something and hear, "Because I didn't know that was what you wanted"? Lack of clear goal setting is a major problem for many employers. Think about it. If your employees don't know what their goals are, how can they meet them? Consequently, they'll never receive credit for doing a good job.

a. ESTABLISH CLEAR GOALS

There are several benefits of establishing clear, quantifiable goals. Specific, measurable goals provide a sense of order and purpose for the entire company. Clear goals allow both employee and manager to develop a broader outlook on company objectives. Once goals are developed, management is better able to make decisions based on company and employee direction. Once goals begin to be achieved, the confidence of both employee and employer is increased.

Goal setting itself is a process that allows managers and employees to continually work for improvement. When goals are set, they should be:

(a) *Specific:* A goal should state "increase sales by 20%" rather than "increase sales." It's important for goals to be measurable and specific. When organizational or departmental goals are unclear, motivation is decreased.

(b) *Mutually agreed upon:* You should strive to have goals mutually set by yourself and the employee. Goals must be mutually agreed upon. Once two people are working toward a common goal, you can be more confident that the goal will be accomplished.

When you are communicating your expectations to your employees you need to state clearly what you want them to do. Misunderstandings increase the risk of criticism for your employees. And, no matter how clear you think your expectations are, someone else may feel otherwise. Understand that, if your expectations are vague, your employees won't say, "Would you please tell me again what you want me to do? I still don't understand." You will have to encourage your employees to ask questions if they have the slightest doubt about what you expect of them.

(c) *Difficult but achievable:* The goals you set should be realistic. They should not be too easy or too difficult; they should be challenging yet attainable.

It may seem that, if your employees agree on a goal, it will be attainable. This, however, is not always the case. Many employees are unwilling to say "I don't think I will be able to accomplish that." This is why you must be in control. You should help employees set goals that are difficult but achievable.

(d) *Comprehensive:* As goals are set they should cover every area of the company's objectives. Goals can be developed for both line and staff activities.

It's very important for you to work with your employees to set goals. Once goals are set, you must work with employees to meet those goals. Often the development of goals goes hand in hand with the development of job standards.

Following are the keys to developing effective goals:

(a) Provide every employee with an up-to-date, clear job description.

(b) Develop job standards so employees know specifically what is expected of them.

(c) Ask each of your employees to develop their own goals rather than developing goals for them.

(d) Set goals that reinforce and coordinate with company goals.

(e) Ensure that both employee and manager clearly understand what will happen when goals are met.

b. CLARIFY JOB DESCRIPTIONS

Some companies work entirely without job descriptions. Others proudly proclaim that they have job descriptions, but upon close examination it becomes clear that these descriptions are sadly antiquated. To be effective at setting goals, it's important that you and your employees first understand clearly the purposes and functions of the jobs they hold. This is where the job description comes in.

If your company does not mandate the use of job descriptions, you can still take it upon yourself, as a manager, to develop a synopsis of your employee's job — with his or her assistance. If you do use job descriptions, it's a useful exercise to verify the accuracy of the job descriptions you're using. Having an up-to-date job description will also prove to be very useful should you later have to hire someone for the position.

In either case, the steps are the same:

1. Ask the employee to outline the key tasks of the job

Many times, even an employee holding a position cannot effectively write down everything that is involved in that position. What's more, you want more than a basic listing of tasks. You want some kind of indication of the importance of each task and how much of the job is spent on that task.

The best way to get at this information is by asking the employee to maintain a log of activities for a period of two to three weeks. This can be a tedious process and isn't often looked upon with a great deal of excitement, but it can be invaluable.

After a three-week period, you and the employee can review the log to pull out major tasks and obtain an indication of how much time is spent on each. This exercise is also a way to spot unnecessary uses of time, duplicated responsibilities, and so on.

2. Write down what you feel the key aspects of the job are

After an employee has held a job for a period of time, the job often changes. Sometimes those changes go unnoticed and, while they may often be positive changes, your employees may head down a road that you don't feel is crucial to the operation of your department or the company.

What do *you* expect of this position and the person holding it?

3. Meet to come up with a consensus

Just because your employee is performing a task that you weren't aware of doesn't mean that task is not necessary or important. And just because you think that something should be done, doesn't mean that it is necessary. By discussing these issues together, you can both overcome misconceptions and misunderstandings. In addition, by involving your employee in this process, you gain his or her commitment to the final job description.

4. Draft the job description

This final step should be an easy one after you've gone through the previous three. Get down each task in writing, describing as clearly as possible what's involved. Also indicate the percentage of time spent on each task. Sample #1 illustrates a job description prepared in this way.

The job description isn't the place to indicate *how* the task is performed or what level of quality you expect. That's where the job standards come into play.

c. ESTABLISH JOB STANDARDS

A job description simply tells *what* tasks are intrinsic to a specific job. This is a crucial step in working toward the establishment of goals, but you need to go one step further by indicating *how* each task must be performed to meet the requirements of the position. You need to develop standards of performance — or job standards. Without standards, performance issues can become extremely fuzzy.

The following example illustrates how such fuzziness can become a problem.

In three weeks it would be time for a review of her graphic designer's job performance and already Linda was getting nervous. She'd had experience in the past reviewing

JOB DESCRIPTION

JOB TITLE	Receptionist
DEPT/DIVISION	Support Services
ACOUNTABLE TO	Support Services Manager
STATUS	Non-exempt
JOB GROUP	C
DATE	8/17/9-

JOB SUMMARY

Receives callers at front desk, determines nature of business and directs callers to appropriate persons. Maintains company general files and mail distribution. Accepts role of "assistant" to the associates who do not have one.

JOB DUTIES AND RESPONSIBILITIES

1. Responsible for performing the duties of an assistant to those associates who do not have one. (5%)

2. Responsible for the scheduling of conference rooms. (1%)

3. Receives visitors and directs to appropriate person. (5%)

4. Maintains company bulletin boards. Responsible for posting and general organization of both boards. (1%)

5. Maintains general filing system on a daily and month-end basis. (2%)

6. Responsible for maintaining the dead file system. (1%)

7. Receives and signs for various deliveries on a daily basis (Pepsi, Mac's Typewriter, Variety Office Products, E.O. Johnson, etc.) (2%)

8. Accommodates for overflow transcription projects. (2%)

9. Opens and distributes daily correspondence mail according to established procedures. (10%)

10. Types correspondence, memos, forms, etc., as needed. (16%)

11. Makes photocopies of materials as needed. Photocopies company schedules weekly. Photocopies product catalogues weekly. (15%)

12. Performs duties of telephone operator as necessary. Operates Horizon Telephone System. (8%)

13. Performs variety of other clerical duties to relieve overflow work in other departments and assists on completion of special projects as assigned by manager (typing, transcription, data entry, word processing, copy jobs, etc.). (22%)

14. Responsible for the subscription and routing system. (2%)

15. Works on Epson PC using WordPerfect 5.0 and Lotus software.

16. Sorts registrations and orders for the Customer Relations Department on a daily basis (processes orders for catalogues). (1%)

17. Responsible for maintaining the mailboxes on Level A. Makes appropriate additions/deletions. (1%)

18. Assists with organization/stocking Level A copy machine and resource area. (1%)

19. Responsible for the paper shredder and daily shredding of confidential information. (10%)

20. Responsible for processing seminar certificates.

21. Responsible for the distribution of promotional brochures.

22. Responsible for maintaining Human Resources library.

23. Performs additional duties as assigned.

ORGANIZATIONAL RELATIONSHIPS

Works with Support Services Manager in maintaining and improving work flow procedures. Will come into contact with almost everyone in the company due to nature of position.

APPROVED BY:

Les R Boss

Manager

_16/5/9-_

Date

I. M. N Change

Director

_16/5/9-_

Date

her graphic designers and copywriters and, unless the review was a good one, she invariably ran into problems.

"What do you mean I'm only performing at a mid-range level? I thought I was doing good work!"

"I can't believe you're only ranking me a 3 out of 5. What do I need to do anyway?"

"How come Julie got an excellent rating and I'm only getting a 'fair'? I thought I was doing a good job."

These were typical of the comments she had heard time and again from the people who worked for her. Or, more correctly, people who used to work for her. The turnover rate in her department had been relatively high. She attributed this to the low pay and lack of advancement opportunities. The real problem? Lack of clear expectations.

The first step in developing job standards is to identify the critical aspects of the job. What elements of the position are necessary to keep the department and the company operating efficiently?

Most jobs have between three and six major areas of responsibilities. When you are trying to pinpoint these responsibilities, don't think of the routine or regular tasks that are performed, but the end result or purpose of those tasks. For instance, in a clerical position, filing would not be a major responsibility. The major responsibility would be "maintaining accurate files that are readily accessible to those who must rely on this information."

Once the areas of responsibility have been identified, three or four standards (or key results) that represent satisfactory performance levels need to be established.

In Linda's case, she determined that the following elements were critical in the graphic designer position:

- Meeting deadlines

- Spending an appropriate amount of time on each project

- Maximizing the effectiveness of the finished piece while staying within budget

It's critical that standards be measurable. If they are not, they become merely subjective indications of how a job should be performed and help neither the employee nor the manager. Effective standards use numbers, time limits, or error/rejection tolerances to establish objective measures of performance. More specifically, managers can use measures of quality, quantity, timeliness, or cost efficiency in establishing standards. Let's take a look at each.

1. Quality

Quality standards are usually written as tolerance for variances from the ideal. In other words, how many errors, omissions, complaints, etc., would you tolerate over a given period of time? Depending on the task being performed, the period of time specified could be anywhere from one hour to one year. One company requires that errors or omissions in payroll changes shall not require special adjustment in more than 1% of all payroll checks issued each month. Another specifies that "phones will be answered prior to the fourth ring. Callers on hold shall be recontacted or connected within one minute. Message forms will include a legible name, number, and time of call."

2. Quantity

Suppose you manage a manufacturing department. A common standard might be, "produce X amount of widgets in X amount of time." This is a measurable standard based on quantity of work produced.

3. Timeliness

Time standards can be written in terms of daily, weekly, monthly, or quarterly deadlines for task completion or amount of turnaround time permitted. For example, one company I know requires project reports to be submitted on the last working day of the month and to include project status, budget to date, problems, causes of problems, and action plan for the next month. Another specifies that all internal correspondence will be ready for distribution not more than 16 working hours after receipt from staff.

4. Cost efficiency

Some positions have responsibility for meeting budgets or affecting costs. Here you would state standards in terms of a maximum dollar budget or a plus or minus variance from that stated budget.

Standards should answer such questions as, "What final results are expected?," "How well must the work be performed?," "How much work must be performed?," "When must the work be performed by?," and so on.

It is important that supervisors refrain from setting arbitrary standards based only on their "gut feelings" of how things should be done. Before specific levels of performance can be established, it is important to identify a baseline of performance. This can be accomplished by asking employees to keep records, by reviewing past performance, or by checking industry standards, if available.

Once baselines have been developed, you can put into place "minimum expected levels of performance." This minimum level becomes the "standard" and defines performance at an *acceptable* level. For instance, if your review scale went from 1 to 5, meeting the standard would give the employee a rating of 3.

Your next step, then, would be to define increments of excellence and increments of unacceptable performance. For each standard you develop you will have to make the determination of what level of performance exceeds your expectations and what level of performance you will not tolerate.

At what level is remedial action in order? At what level will the employee be terminated?

The levels that you develop need to be clear to both you and your employees. These standards will vary from manager to manager — from organization to organization. That's all right. *But* the standards should *never* vary from one employee to another within the same job. Standards need to be applied consistently to all employees.

d. INVOLVING EMPLOYEES IN GOAL SETTING

Goals should not be developed in isolation and then handed down to employees as edicts. Employees need to be involved in the goal-setting process. They will be more willing to work toward achievement of goals if they have been allowed to give input based on their personal experiences and aspirations. It is a standard management principle: commitment is engendered from involvement.

Goal development in isolation or failure to pay heed to the input of your employees are both good ways to sabotage your efforts in this area.

e. THE THREE ASPECTS OF GOAL SETTING THAT ARE OFTEN OVERLOOKED

1. Coordinating individual with company goals

An employee's life is not segmented into two distinct parts: one part which runs from 5:00 p.m. to 8:00 a.m. and the other which runs from 8:01 a.m. to 4:59 p.m. An employee's life extends beyond the office — personal and professional goals are integrally intertwined. Your efforts at setting goals need to focus on personal goal achievement as well as professional achievement.

2. Coordinating company and employee goals

Just as you cannot successfully develop employee goals without considering personal goals, you cannot develop employee goals without considering company goals. If the employee's efforts are not directed at tasks and goals that are aligned with a company's goals, nothing has been accomplished. The employee is not being productive.

Sometimes a manager will have goals that are divergent from the company's goals and, to meet his or her own personal agenda, will have employees working toward a different end than the end the company envisions. This is always a mistake. Be sure that you know your company's goals and that you are communicating them to your employees. Be sure that their goals and the company's goals are working toward the same end.

3. Spelling out the consequences of not meeting goals

What are the consequences of not meeting a goal? A lower rating on the employee evaluation form? A written warning? Suspension? Termination? There must be a consequence associated with failure to meet goals. If there is no consequence, your employees will soon feel that it really makes no difference whether they do what you ask. Be sure that you've communicated the impact of not meeting goals and be sure that you follow through in the event that goals are not met.

f. ADDITIONAL CONSIDERATIONS

Here are some additional points you should consider when working with your employees on developing goals and standards:

1. Don't keep the goals a secret

The most important element of establishing goals in the first place is to help employees understand what's expected of them so they can monitor their own performance. Make sure that you communicate goals to your employees, make sure they understand them, and make sure they know what you have determined as an unacceptable level of performance.

2. Make sure the goals are written

For some reason, committing goals to writing makes it much more likely that they will be remembered and met. Make sure that you and your employees have written goals.

3. Let employees participate in the measurement of their jobs

Again, don't establish an air of secrecy around the job standards you develop. Let employees assist in keeping track of their goal accomplishment. Give them ready access to your records of their performance. Allow them the opportunity to explain unusual circumstances, if necessary.

4. Give frequent progress reports or let them generate these reports on their own

Keep employees informed of their progress on an ongoing basis. Remember, your primary goal is to avoid surprises at review time.

5. Allow some tolerance for error

Nobody performs at 100% all of the time. Don't set unrealistic expectations for your employees or make the highest category of performance ranking an impossible target.

g. CONCLUSION

Relationships are strengthened when people know what to expect from each other. No company can function without goals. There is nothing more frustrating to employees than not knowing how their jobs contribute to the overall working of the company. By establishing specific, quantifiable, and obtainable goals, you're taking the first step toward recognition of employee accomplishments.

5
COMMUNICATION

The development and establishment of clear, realistic, and measurable goals is an important element in maintaining a motivated workforce. Establishing goals isn't enough, however. Those goals must be clearly communicated and that communication must become a continuous process.

One of the basic tenets of McGregor's Theory Y, discussed in chapter 1, is: "People are important." And, what's one of the best ways to let people *know* they're important? Tell them.

Communication, whether for praise, criticism, or information, is an important motivational factor. It's amazing, then, that while we're in the midst of an "information explosion" our organizational communications are so often faulty or ineffective.

a. WHAT YOU SHOULD TELL EMPLOYEES

An organization needs to communicate to promote understanding, productivity, and a team identity. As a manager or supervisor, you need to communicate —

(a) the rules and policies of the organization,

(b) information on current organizational activities,

(c) reviews of past results, mistakes in judgment, and goal accomplishment, and

(d) progress, organizational plans, and corporate objectives.

Why should you tell your employees these things? Because involvement is an important determinant of productivity. If your people don't know where the company's going, where it's been, or why you're asking them to do certain things, they can't be productive. They have no idea of how what they do fits into the "whole picture." Your job is to give them an idea of how they fit in. Then you need to keep giving them that information so they will continue to produce.

A manager's job is 90% communication. It's not hard to understand, then, why poor communication is a major business problem today. Poor communication is at the root of almost every business problem from low productivity to employee theft. Communication is the giving and receiving of information needed for intelligent action or decision. It is also an act of creating understanding between individuals.

There can be several reasons for poor communication. It may be the result of ego or self-interest. You may feel that certain things are not important enough to communicate. Or perhaps listening is the problem; because we all prefer to talk rather than listen, efforts to communicate may not get heard or we may incorrectly interpret the things we hear. Perhaps the most deep-rooted barrier to communication, however, is simply the failure to see the need for it.

Lack of proper communication has far-reaching effects for any business. These effects may include the following:

(a) Good ideas that are not implemented because they were not heard

(b) Errors that result from miscommunication

(c) Lowered productivity when managers do not motivate subordinates enough in communicating

(d) Increased employee turnover brought on by inadequate manager-subordinate communication

b. COMMUNICATION PROBLEMS

We all have a hard time spotting the problems in our own communication styles. There are, however, several common problem areas that many managers suffer from. Perhaps you can spot some of your personal problem areas here.

1. Hearing only what you expect to hear

When dealing with the day-to-day aspects of a job, it is all too easy to begin to assume you've heard it all. When one of your employees or a coworker is speaking to you, you may simply nod your head with a knowing smile. You think you know what they're going to say next.

Alternatively, you may consciously (or unconsciously) ignore information that you didn't expect to hear. The classic example of this is the standard greeting "How are you?" How often have you really listened to the answer instead of expecting the response to be "fine."

Here are some other common questions you may ask your employees without really listening to their responses:

"How's it going?"

"How was your weekend?"

"Having a busy day?"

"What did you think of _____?"

What do you think happens when you assume you already *know* what your employees have to say? They start giving you the canned answers you expect. They know you're not going to listen to what they say anyway. So you'll hear something like:

"How's it going?"

"Fine."

"No problem?"

"No."

"Great. Keep up the good work."

"Sure."

You go back to your office thinking you're a great communicator. But one day, someone tells you you're a poor communicator. "What!" you explode. "I talk to my employees every day! We've got a great relationship."

Or one of your best employees suddenly gives notice. You had no idea this person was unhappy. Every day when you asked "How're things going?" you'd receive the answer of "Fine."

What's going on?

You have to stop trying to second-guess the people that work for you and start *listening*. There's nothing more dismotivating to an employee than to feel no one is listening. They don't want to be paid ear-service by a preoccupied, self-centered manager.

2. Letting biases interfere

It's unfortunate, but biases exist in every aspect of our on-the-job relationships. If you like somebody, you're more likely to listen to what he or she has to say than if you dislike this person. In fact, even negative information is more readily accepted from those we like and respect.

Biases also affect the way we view the information we're being given. Would you pay close attention to a marginal employee who wants to discuss reworking some technical aspect of the company's procedures?

Nobody is completely unbiased. We each have our own quirks — our individual likes and dislikes. These attitudes developed during childhood, adolescence, or young adulthood. Fortunately, you don't have to be the victim of your biases. Try the following:

(a) Become aware of your feelings. Ask yourself how your background — age, sex, race, ethnicity — might

52

be affecting your perceptions of people who are different from you.

(b) Minimize differences by understanding and accepting them. Look for a common ground from which you can form the basis for good communication. Take the time to find out what the other person's expectations are and adjust your approach to suit the situation.

(c) Find out how your behavior is influencing others. Be up-front. If you're having a hard time communicating with someone in your department, tell them you're having problems.

Biases can go beyond stereotypes. One bad experience with an employee can color your future relationship — if you let it. Remember, first impressions do count, and second, and third...

Your actions and attitudes can also create a biased image in the eyes of your employees. Are you aware of the image you project and the effect that image has on your relationship with your employees?

3. Semantics

The English language is very difficult to learn because of the great number of words with similar meanings. Even native English speakers can experience misunderstandings.

What do the phrases, "He's got a good track record," or "I couldn't get to first base," mean to you? What might these same phrases mean to an athletics coach?

Betty Lehan Harragan's *Games Mother Never Taught You* (Rawson Associates, 1977) tells us that the business world is full of sports and armed service expressions. Traditionally, experiences in sports and the armed services have been primarily male experiences. When business speech is peppered with phrases from these two arenas, it can be confusing, sometimes even misleading, to those, particularly women, who don't share that background. In addition, each type of business has its own language.

Your attempts to communicate effectively with your employees can be severely hampered if you're using language that they don't understand.

4. Noise

Noise can be internal or external. It's a major factor contributing to poor communication. Since we process information much faster than we deliver information, it's easy to let our minds wander. This is even more likely to happen as we're bombarded on all sides by competing noise.

There are times when your employees need your undivided attention. At times like these you need to do everything possible to eliminate all competing noise. You should have your calls held, put up the "Do Not Disturb" sign — even leave the building, if necessary.

5. Emotions

Our mood also determines how well we listen. If we're relaxed, we'll absorb more. If we've had a rough day, we won't pay close attention.

As we've seen, honesty is often the best way to approach the people you deal with. Let them know when it's not a good time to talk to you. Be polite, but be firm. If it's not a good time, make an appointment for later.

c.   NON-VERBAL COMMUNICATION

Many managers fail to take into consideration the importance of non-verbal communication. In fact, non-verbal cues are an important part of human communication. If we don't pay attention to body language, we may not get the full message. Poor interpretation of non-verbal messages can cause many problems. Consider the following example.

An 11th-century Scandinavian story tells of a debate that took place between a one-eyed Viking and a holy man. Each communicated only with gestures. At one point in the silent debate the holy man raised a single finger. The Viking responded by raising two fingers. The holy man then replied with three raised fingers. At this, the Viking raised a fist and the debate ended.

A spectator asked the holy man to explain what the gestures had meant. "I raised one finger," he responded, " to indicate that God is one. My opponent disputed me by displaying two fingers to show that besides God, the Father, there is also God, the Son. To let him know that his theology was incomplete I raised three fingers because there is a Godly Trinity: Father, Son, and Holy Spirit. But this man is a fine debater. When he made a fist to show that the Trinity is one in God, I could not argue any further."

When the Viking was asked for his version of the debate he said, "It had nothing at all to do with God. When my opponent raised one finger he was mocking me because I have only one eye. I countered with two fingers to indicate that my one eye is the equal of his two. He continued to laugh at me by raising three fingers to show that between us we have only three eyes. I then raised a fist to let him know what he could expect if he persisted in mocking me."

The spoken word is a major mode of communication — yet it is by no means the only one. Non-verbal communication also plays a vital role in our interactions with others. Some of the most common types of non-verbal behavior are familiar to us all. A nod of the head, a wave of the hand, a frown; any of these behaviors will convey a message.

We use our entire body when we speak. Some people gesture a great deal. Others give different messages because of the rigidity of their bodies.

Here are a few tips to help you improve your non-verbal communication skills.

(a) It's very difficult to read somebody you don't know well. You need to be familiar with their typical reactions. Get to know your staff members and start to note their body language.

(b) It's helpful to know the background of a situation. What has just happened? What would your reaction be? Some facial expressions are very close — consider the expressions for fear and surprise. Therefore, we may make incorrect assumptions unless we are aware of the situation.

(c) Since emotions are very fleeting, you must be able to pick up very rapid expressions. Keep in mind that many facial expressions are blends of two or more feelings.

(d) When possible, check your interpretations of non-verbal cues. This can help avoid misunderstandings.

d. ORGANIZATIONAL BARRIERS TO POSITIVE COMMUNICATIONS

Over time, organizations develop very predictable patterns of communication. Many of these communication patterns are poor. Poor communication occurs because of three major problem areas.

1. Overload

How many pieces of paper cross your desk each day? How many memos, letters, reports, and journals? How many people stop by to ask you questions, to provide you with information or to chat?

It's just as bad for the people who work for you. Consider the many different kinds of messages you give to your employees each day — some verbal, some written, some non-verbal — many conflicting. Consider the messages they're also getting from others in your organization. It's no wonder they have a difficult time piecing all the information together.

2. Using the wrong medium

Have you ever made a verbal request that was never acted upon? Have you ever committed something to paper you later realized would have been better handled in person? Have you ever called a meeting and found that you ended up wasting the time of two or more key people?

The medium is as important as the message in the business world. Often, the medium dictates whether the message is heard, understood, and acted upon.

In communicating praise, for instance, a verbal "good job" is effective. A written letter of commendation may be even more effective. A verbal public acknowledgment may be the most effective of all.

3. Failure to "close"

In sales, the goal of the salesperson is to close the sale — to ask for the order. In short, to receive positive feedback.

In communicating with our employees, we often fail to close the conversation. We call a meeting and never make a decision about who is going to do what. If we do make assignments, we don't follow up to see how our employees are progressing. If we find out that progress is being made, we often fail to provide the positive feedback. We fail to close.

The result? Miscommunication.

e. A THREE-STAGE APPROACH TO AVOIDING MISCOMMUNICATION

There is probably no more important (and more often overlooked) key to effective performance in the business world than good communication skills. But even in an atmosphere of cooperativeness, messages can be misunderstood and problems can develop. Following is a three-stage approach for avoiding miscommunication through verification, clarification, and follow-up.

1. Verification

Verification is defined by Webster as "testing the truth or accuracy" of something. People very often do not wait until they have all the information they need before forming an opinion. In conversations especially, we're often "thinking ahead" because we can listen at a much faster rate than we can speak.

Verification takes place whether you're giving or receiving a message and involves very basic questions. Here are some examples.

When receiving: "So you're saying that. . . "

"I hear you saying. . . "

"Let me make sure I understand you."

When giving: "I want to make sure you understand what I mean. Could you tell me how you interpreted what I just said."

In both cases you want to verify that the communication has been perceived accurately. At first it may seem somewhat awkward to be asking these questions. Once you have done it for a while, however, you'll find that it comes more naturally. The value of avoiding problems and complications in the future far outweighs a little discomfort initially.

2. Clarification

To clarify is to make clear. This stage involves questioning when you're receiving information and explaining when you're giving information. It's the natural follow-up to stage one, especially in those instances where the message being sent is not being understood clearly.

Many of us are hesitant to ask too many questions for fear that we'll appear stupid. Consider how much more "stupid" you'll appear if you do something incorrectly or take the wrong action because you failed to clarify in the first place.

On the other hand, when you're giving information be aware of this natural hesitance. Encourage the other person to ask questions so that you know you're getting your point across accurately.

At the end of any discussion make sure that both you and the other party (or parties) understand what should happen next, if anything, or what decisions have been made. By taking extra steps to make things clear you can avoid misunderstandings later.

3. Follow-up

Have you ever attended a meeting where it seemed that everything was going quite well, good decisions were being made, and discussion about steps to take in the future seemed clear and understood — but then there was never any follow-up and nothing really developed from the discussion? That's what often happens with our conversations. We make some decisions, identify a course of action to pursue, but never follow up. This is a critical area that you can learn to control.

For instance, following a meeting on budget preparation, you might sum up as follows: "Okay, now, June, you'll be gathering figures on XYZ and will have them prepared by December 1. Jack, you'll be looking into ABC and will have a report to me by November 15. We'll be meeting again on December 15 to wrap this up. Any questions?"

At the clarification stage, set a time to follow up on the discussion if follow-up is appropriate. Then *do it*.

Here are some additional tips to help you avoid miscommunication:

(a) Avoid making such comments as "you don't understand" during the clarification stage. Such statements can result in defensive reactions. Instead you could say something like, "I don't think I'm making myself clear. What I meant is…"

(b) Don't let personal biases interfere with the quality of your listening. Recognize that an attractive, charming person or somebody you like personally will be easier for you to understand than someone you find difficult to listen to because of their physical appearance, speaking ability, or your negative feelings toward them. In cases where you realize you may be biased against a person, make an extra effort to stay alert.

(c) Avoid daydreaming. Because we can listen at a rate of 400 to 600 wpm but speak at fewer than 200 wpm, there is a great tendency to let our minds wander when someone is speaking to us. Instead, make a special effort to listen to what's being said.

(d) Use "I" messages when giving criticism. Take responsibility rather than trying to place blame (even inadvertently) on the other person. For instance, "I feel confused" is better than "You're confusing me."

f. COMMUNICATION VEHICLES

Whether your organization is large or small, it can sometimes become cumbersome to get news out to the people who need it when they need it. Following are some suggestions of "communication vehicles" that can help you keep your staff informed:

1. Rap sessions

Do you ever get the feeling that all the people around you want to do is gripe? Maybe you need to set up some form of regular rap session. They may need a way to air their grievances.

Especially in the rank and file, opportunities for airing opinions, expressing concerns, or voicing displeasure are limited. These employees are not allowed the input granted to upper or even middle management. Sometimes all they really need is a chance to get together and rap.

Rap sessions can be either formal (structured) or informal (unstructured). The type you choose will depend on the climate of your organization. If you're aware of a great deal of employee hostility you might decide to use a structured form of rap session. You should select a chairperson, schedule regular meetings with specific topics of discussion for the agenda, and be certain to have representatives of management present at these sessions.

If, however, the climate of your organization is relatively peaceful, unstructured rap sessions may work wonderfully. You might still suggest topics of discussion and have management representation; however these sessions would need less monitoring and less control.

Hyman Ltée, a pulp processing machinery producer in Quebec, has made a conscious decision to decentralize decision making. The company has developed a unique type of "rap session" which includes customers as well as employees. Employees, from order clerk to senior management, forge ties with clients in sessions where clients are able to express their concerns about the company's products and services, and employees are able to play an integral role in responding to these comments and working toward positive solutions. It's a step beyond the traditional *internal* rap sessions — a step that allows employees to assume greater responsibility for customer service on a front-line level. Customer input has led to improvements in invoicing procedures, equipment packaging, inventory assortment, and quality control.

2. Regular meetings

Meetings are sometimes cursed, yet they are a vital part of the formal communication structure. Regular department meetings in addition to regular meetings with individual department members should be part of your communication improvement program.

These meetings are a perfect time to discuss the issues of rules and policies, current organizational activities, past results, and future plans.

3. Grievance or suggestion system

A Connecticut manufacturer is said to have started the first suggestion system in 1880. It wasn't until the late 1930s and WWII, though, that suggestion systems became widespread. Today, in some companies, the proportion of accepted ideas runs as high as 50%.

Most companies make a half-hearted attempt to establish a grievance system. Sometimes it's a formal procedure set up in the employee handbook, or it may be a suggestion box placed somewhere in the building. If your employees feel that your attempts are half-hearted, however, all of your efforts are useless.

Certainly you should encourage employees to express concerns and complaints directly to their managers. However, you should also realize that there will always be times an employee simply will not feel comfortable talking to his or her immediate manager. That's why you need a formal grievance procedure. That's also why you may need a suggestion box.

Granted, some of the anonymous complaints you get may seem vicious and non-constructive. Behind every vicious complaint, though, is an unhappy employee. And unhappy employees can spread discontent.

Never dismiss a complaint, regardless of how insignificant you think it might be. If you do, you risk —

(a) employees feeling that you "don't care" what they think,

(b) letting a small problem become a big problem that could take months to solve, and

(c) creating misunderstandings that you could have resolved.

For your suggestion system to work, you must let employees know what suggestions you have received and what action you intend to take. Many companies also establish reward systems for particularly useful suggestions.

A report prepared by the U.S. Small Business Administration entitled *An Employee Suggestion System For Small Companies* lists five elements of an effective employee suggestion system:

(a) A suggestion box to keep employees reminded of the plan and to receive their ideas

(b) An administrator to gather suggestions, obtain evaluations from operating officials concerned, and otherwise see to the smooth functioning of the suggestion system

(c) A committee to consider suggestions and approve awards

(d) Recognition and rewards for ideas that are accepted and suitable explanations for those that are not

(e) A follow-up system to see that good ideas are put to use, either immediately or whenever changing conditions make them applicable

4. Open-door policies

Being available to your employees and letting them know that you are available is half the battle in developing good communications. Having an open-door policy, though, means more than having your door open. It means being ready to *listen* when your employees come to you with suggestions, problems or complaints.

Jim Smith, President of Maritime Travel in Halifax, stays close to his employees by making a circuit of his 28 east coast offices every six to eight weeks. His gauge of management effectiveness isn't market share and revenue, it's staff retention and morale.

At Computer Output Printing Incorporated in Houston, CEO Andy Plata asks new employees to write him letters. Before new people come to work, Plata and his managers ask them to write a letter to management about why they've chosen to work there. After the first week they're asked to write another letter describing "what they hope to accomplish at COPI and what contributions they feel they can make." Seven weeks later they write a third letter outlining their progress. The letters become the focus of managers' discussions on goal setting and the improvement of work relations.

When you make yourself available to your subordinates, you are emphasizing supportiveness, receptivity, and participation. You increase the likelihood that the information your employees receive is accurate information and you increase motivation.

Naturally, you won't accept or use every idea or suggestion that comes your way. The fact that you are there to listen with an open mind means a great deal. Your employees don't want to hear, "We tried that before and it didn't work." On the other hand, they don't have to hear, "That's a wonderful idea. We'll do it immediately." They *should* hear, "Thank you for the suggestion. I appreciate every comment you make because it lets me know how concerned you are with the company and that's important. You matter. You're important."

There are also benefits to you in having an open-door policy:

(a) You will get to find out what's going on in the rank and file. You will become part of the grapevine, a very powerful position to be in.

(b) You will know about minor problems before they become big ones. Then you can begin corrective action immediately.

(c) You will be able to encourage a team spirit among your employees. You will be influencing them directly — not merely in an advisory capacity.

An open door does not mean that you can be interrupted any time. It may mean that you can be seen by appointment only. It may mean that you're available during certain times of the day. It is important, however, that you aren't frequently unavailable or too busy to be approached.

5. Opinion surveys

Don't just sit around wondering what your employees have on their minds. Ask them. Employee surveys are a quick, effective means of gathering information from employees in every area of the company. You won't be able to know who said what, but you will be able to get a good, overall feel for company-wide attitudes and perceptions.

Two important points need to be made here:

(a) Don't conduct opinion surveys too often. It reduces their effectiveness and may make employees think you don't know what you're doing.

(b) Share the results with your employees.

6. Social gatherings

Special events and company-sponsored parties are good ways to open up communication channels. The relaxed atmosphere at these gatherings makes them a good place for a free exchange of casual information.

At social gatherings you are able to do the following:

(a) Get to know employees and their families more personally. Understanding the personal aspects of your employees' lives can help you understand their goals, aspirations, and motivations.

(b) Observe the casual interactions among employees. Who speaks to whom? Often these casual friendships give you clues to the informal communication network of your organization.

(c) Relate non-defensively to problem employees. Social events can sometimes provide you with just the opportunity to get closer to a difficult worker.

Never underestimate the power or value of the organizational grapevine. And *never* try to stop it. For one thing, you won't be able to do it. For another, the grapevine is a vital form of informal communication. In fact, recent studies have indicated that the information carried through the grapevine is approximately 80% accurate. If you're not already a part of the grapevine, you should make an attempt to become a part of it.

The importance of good organizational communication can't be emphasized enough. As a manager committed to the positive motivation of your employees, you should make a sincere effort to do the following:

(a) Listen.

(b) Use feedback. Make sure that what you think you heard is actually the message the sender intended you to receive.

(c) Comment on non-verbal cues you're picking up, especially if you're getting mixed messages.

(d) Physically remove yourself from noise factors that can hurt the communication process. Leave the building if necessary.

(e) Use face-to-face communication whenever possible. You'll be able to take advantage of non-verbal input you don't get over the phone. You'll also avoid misunderstandings that can occur in writing.

(f) Be a committed listener. Don't allow your mind to wander.

(g) Be open minded. Don't let personal biases interfere with the message you're being sent.

(h) Make notes, especially if you've agreed to do something or need to take some kind of future action.

(i) Be aware of your own reactions.

Communication plays a very special role in any business relationship. Good communication requires the desire to make the effort and the skill to communicate effectively. It's up to you to make that effort and develop the skill.

6
POSITIVE FEEDBACK

"How am I doing?"

This was the well-known query presented to citizens of New York for many years by their mayor, Ed Koch. He wanted to know if he was doing a good job, so he asked. He would ask through the media. He'd ask in his formal presentations to the city. And he'd ask in one-on-one situations with citizens he met throughout the city.

We've already discussed the fact that your employees want to know how they're doing. Unfortunately, they probably don't have the confidence or the alacrity that Mayor Koch had to actually come to you and pose the question. Still, they're dying to know. And it's up to you to tell them.

Most companies have formal systems in place to provide employee evaluations. Usually these evaluations take place twice a year. But while these evaluation meetings serve an important purpose, they don't fulfill an employee's need for consistent and constant feedback. You need to do more than tell them every six months that they're doing a good (or a bad) job.

What can happen if you don't? Plenty. Let's look at a couple of examples.

Nancy started her job as a secretary for a small company five years ago. She was well liked, even though her performance wasn't all it could be. Because of her good personality and the family-like structure of the company she was kept on, shifted from one job to another where her skills could be best utilized. For a time she was a receptionist because she was good on the phones. Then she served as assistant for a few people because she followed instructions well and was pleasant to work with.

During this time, Nancy was never told that her typing skills were below par. She was never told that her letter and report compositions were inadequate. She was never given the opportunity to improve. Eventually, the company grew beyond her limited means and, when it was no longer possible to find positions that were suitable for her, she was terminated. Neither Nancy nor her coworkers saw it coming and they didn't understand when it happened. The termination was a troublesome one — for Nancy, for her managers, and for her fellow employees. Long after she was gone they suffered from feelings of insecurity. "If it could happen to her, it could happen to me." "How can I tell if I'm really doing a good job?" were comments heard throughout the firm time and time again.

Had Nancy been told of her inadequacies at an early date she could have been trained in the areas where she was lacking. She could have grown with the company and been a valued and loyal employee. Because this didn't happen, the company was forced to let her go — on acrimonious terms.

You owe it to your employees to provide feedback not only so you can get the most productive use of them but also so they can develop their skills and grow with you.

Good employees can also be lost due to inattention.

Linda was also hired as a secretary at a small firm and grew with the company to eventually hold a management position. She took courses at a local college to enhance her skills, joined numerous professional groups to establish her professionalism, and worked hard. Her managers valued her contributions and felt she was a model employee — but they never felt the need to tell her because she always seemed to be "self-motivated." Because Linda never heard the positive comments she craved, she felt unappreciated. She felt that because she had been promoted from within and not hired as an "expert" from the outside, eventually she would be replaced. She began to look for employment elsewhere and eventually left the company. The day she resigned was the first time she was told just how important she was to the company. Unfortunately, by then it was too late.

Feedback, whether positive or negative, is traditionally difficult for managers to provide to their employees. Why? Quite probably because parents also have a hard time with giving appropriate feedback to their children and few of us have ever learned how to do it effectively. Let's take a look at how we can provide both positive and negative feedback more effectively to our employees.

a. GIVING POSITIVE FEEDBACK — HOW TO RECOGNIZE YOUR EMPLOYEES

Suppose you have an employee who meets all of your expectations and does the job exactly right but isn't a stellar performer. You feel insincere about going out of your way to tell this employee what a great job she or he is doing.

Well, positive recognition can be more subtle than blatantly praising an employee for doing a good job — sometimes it requires little more than recognizing the employee's efforts. Let's look at some examples.

Sam has worked at ABC Corporation for 25 years. During that time he's had a series of managers. None have ever noticed (or recognized) him for performing any better than the other 10 members of his work group.

A new manager was recently hired. After reviewing production reports and individual evaluations of worker performance, the new manager is surprised to see that Sam was a high performer during his first 13 years of employment. His performance declined, though, after his 13th year. He now works at a fair but steady pace that could most accurately be termed satisfactory.

The new manager calls Sam into her office to talk, not about his performance, but about his interests (at home and at work). She wants to know about the things he likes about his job and about the things he dislikes. After the meeting she remarks, "Sam, your records indicate that you have consistently been one of ABC's best employees. I hope you will keep up the good work."

She continues these individual meetings and always makes a special effort to comment on any increase in Sam's output. In a relatively short period of time, Sam's level of performance is exceeding the point it had been at 12 years earlier!

Sam was recognized.

Suzanne was excellent in her position as sales clerk in a large department store. In fact, she was so good that she was quickly promoted to the position of women's wear sales manager. In this position she was responsible for a large staff of other sales clerks.

As sales manager, however, Suzanne quickly lost the drive she had had as a clerk. She no longer felt the personal reward that accompanied a large sale. She was also growing envious of others in her department who seemed to get all the credit while she merely monitored results.

One day Suzanne had the opportunity to speak to the store manager about this problem. The store manager listened closely and assured Suzanne that her problem wasn't unique. Several other department sales managers felt very much the same way.

A few weeks later the store manager called all the managers together. He told them about a new program the store was implementing: sales teams. Each department manager would be responsible for a team of salespeople. Managers were responsible for encouraging and motivating members of their team to increase sales. After a three-month trial period a reward system would be established. Each month a specific department would be recognized for outstanding sales achievement.

The new system was, in effect, no different from the old system. The store manager had been smart enough to realize that it wasn't enough for department sales managers to watch their staff succeed. Managers needed to feel that they played an important part in this achievement.

Six months later the store's sales had increased dramatically. Department sales managers felt better about the work they were doing and the role they played in improving sales. Department members felt part of a team with a clear goal in mind. The monthly reward dinners were also well accepted. In short...

They were recognized too.

If you want to get the same kind of action and see the same results from the people you manage, you should recognize them: frequently...sincerely...and consistently.

If you think about it, we're all trying to be recognized, whether we're putting on a new suit or presenting a major proposal. When you're dealing with employees, recognition is extremely important. In fact, almost every aspect of employee reward — monetary or nonmonetary — is a function of recognition.

Everyone likes recognition. There are some important points that should be raised, though. The effect of recognition on employees depends on —

(a) what they are recognized for,

(b) how they are recognized, and

(c) how often they are recognized.

It's your responsibility to examine these variables and determine how they apply to each of your employees. Remember, what you recognize an employee for and how you recognize that employee are as important as providing recognition in the first place.

b. GIVING CREDIT AND PRAISE FOR ACCOMPLISHMENT

What happens when employees in your department meet or exceed the goals you have set?

Your answer should be "I praise them."

If your answer is "nothing" or "the achievement of the goal should be reward enough," don't be surprised if motivation is low.

There is no such thing as a "self-motivator." Each of us is motivated by something and for many of us that something is praise.

Fail to praise your employees and they will fail to perform. They will fail to perform time after time after time until you will either replace them or they will seek employment elsewhere. The end result, of course, is that you have lost a potentially good employee.

We all like appreciation. We like to feel needed and wanted. Work takes up a great deal of our time each day. It's not surprising, then, that praise for the things we accomplish at work is so important to our self-esteem.

If any of your employees tell you that they don't need to be appreciated, you can be 100% sure that they are lying. Author Laurence Peter said, "There are two kinds of egotists: those who admit it and the rest of us." With that in mind, let's consider how you can recognize employees who are consistently meeting or exceeding their work goals.

"John is such a good employee I don't need to tell him what a good job he's doing. He just knows."

Don't be so sure about it.

Many companies demonstrate a lack of positive reinforcement or praise. Countless managers take the attitude that if employees are doing a good job, they know they're doing a good job. It's the employees who aren't performing effectively that get the recognition — negative recognition. The star performers are often, in effect, ignored.

Then, one day, when their performance starts to decline, their managers will shake their heads perplexedly and say, "I just don't understand it. He (or she) used to be such a good employee. I don't understand what went wrong. I hardly had to pay any attention to him (or her) at all. He (or she) was a self-starter."

And there's the problem. There's no such thing as never having to pay attention to an employee. In fact, it's often your star performers that really need that extra attention, because they are performing for a reason. Often that reason is the search for recognition or praise.

According to Abraham Koman, the higher the worker's perception of personal competence, the higher the level of performance will be. In *Industrial and Organizational Psychology*, he indicates that:

- Employees who are told they are incompetent will perform worse than those who are told they are competent

- Self-perceived ability based on previous performance is positively related to later performance

- The more a person has failed in the past, the less he or she will try to achieve later

- Groups that have failed set goals that increase the probability of failing again

74

- People with low self-esteem are less likely to achieve difficult goals they have set for themselves than individuals of high self-esteem

Managers must always ask themselves, "What is my action (or inaction) saying to subordinates about what is of secondary or no importance to me?" Managers need to make sure that each person in the organization knows they have a unique contribution to make.

When do you offer praise? The answer to this question relates directly to establishing employee goals. You offer praise when an employee has met or exceeded one of the requirements you have established together.

When you offer praise, make sure that it is —

- immediate
- specific
- sincere
- consistent

The question of immediacy is one that relates directly to performance review. When you keep a log of employee accomplishments to cover at a yearly review, how much impact do you think it will have on an employee's performance? Very little.

However, when you consistently note and comment on achievements and accomplishments *as soon as they happen*, the effect on morale and productivity is substantial.

It's also important to be specific when offering praise to employees. If your administrative assistant stays late to finish an important report and you mumble "good job" as you rush out the door, is your assistant to assume that the report is well formatted, the report was prepared in a timely manner, or the report contained few typographical errors?

In fact, your assistant will have no idea what you mean *unless you say what you mean*. "Thank you for staying late to finish this report. I appreciated your dedication and dependability." That would tell your assistant specifically what you mean by "good job."

Sincerity is crucial when offering praise to employees. The people that work for you will be able to tell immediately if your comments are sincere or meaningless. Giving praise simply because you know you should is not enough. You need to be giving praise because you honestly believe that a good job was done.

c. DEVELOPING EFFECTIVE REWARD SYSTEMS

Mary Kay Ash has constructed a giant multi-million dollar cosmetics empire. On Awards Night, 8000 women who sell Mary Kay cosmetics are rewarded with applause, praise, and gifts ranging from pocket calculators to pink Cadillacs. Queens of sales and recruitment are crowned and presented with flowers and scepters.

Your efforts to reward employees need not be so elaborate. In fact, employee award systems can be as simple as —

- an "employee of the month" or "secretary of the year" award,

- special clubs for high performers,

- a new job title,

- publicity in the company newsletter or local paper,

- certificates of appreciation, or

- status symbols, such as a private parking space or a special office location.

As you can see, reward systems can come in many shapes and sizes. Yet, as we've already seen, praise as well as criticism is difficult for many supervisors to provide. Most managers don't provide even the simple rewards that could maintain the enthusiasm and commitment of their employees. However, properly provided, rewards can boost morale, strengthen motivation, and increase productivity. They are a very effective way to get good performance and innovative ideas from employees.

1. Awards

As one manager comments, "Awards serve as a sort of corporate Nobel prize, acknowledging in a very tangible way that the corporation recognizes, appreciates, and rewards the outstanding contributions of its employees."

The awards themselves do not serve as motivators. In fact, employees will probably not work harder just to receive an award. Awards do, however, serve as evidence that an employee's efforts are appreciated.

By establishing an award system or simply providing rewards, the company sends a clear message to employees — a message that says the organization recognizes, values, and rewards extraordinary effort, innovative thinking, and exceptional skills. The employees who receive the rewards will become role models for others in the company.

The way you present an award may vary. An award may be issued in the form of a private "thank you" from the employee's supervisor or a plaque, desk set, gift certificate, or other token may be presented. You may even wish to make the presentation a major event.

Whatever you decide to do, remember that it is essential that some publicity be present. Without it, you lose an important opportunity to highlight the kind of behavior you'd like to see in others. You also lose the opportunity to establish role models for others.

Ross Laboratories in Columbus, Ohio implemented a rather unusual recognition program in 1987. Created by President Dick Gast, the program was devised to reward "excellence" demonstrated by employees. Because excellence is such a subjective term, Ross decided that all employees should participate in the process of defining and recognizing it.

The program has three levels of achievement with awards for each level. Level I winners are announced at a general meeting where each winner receives a two-ounce silver ingot engraved with the Ross award of excellence logo on the front and the original Ross milk truck logo on the back. Then, Level II winners are chosen from this group and they receive a five-ounce ingot in the shape of an Olympic-style medal, encased in a black velvet-covered box. They also receive a letter of congratulations from the division president and attend a recognition dinner which is held at the end of each year. At the end of the fourth quarter, another election is held to select Level III winners who receive a three-day trip and a $250 gift certificate to celebrate their achievements.

Any full-time employee can nominate another full-time employee for an award — they may even nominate themselves. Nominations are considered by a screening committee of workers from each functional area. Mike Strapp, chairman of the excellence award committee, feels that while paychecks can motivate, recognition from one's coworkers encourages employees to aspire to further personal and professional goals.

When well managed, awards programs can encourage innovation, dedication, and productivity.

2. Problems with awards

Providing employees with awards does present some problems, however. A common concern is that rewarding employees in even a small way can lead to competition and jealousy. Letting this concern keep you from offering awards to outstanding employees is unnecessary, however. To deal with possible jealousies, companies have tried the following:

(a) Giving individual awards to all members of a project team so that no individual feels slighted

(b) Structuring the award system so that awards go only to those whose achievements are outstanding and widely recognized

In addition to competition and jealousy, there is another concern: the decision to grant or withhold an award is an employment decision. As such, it is subject to all of the laws, regulations, and guidelines that apply to any other type of employment decision. Consequently, with any type of program you establish, it is important that you —

(a) require a review of awards by the employee relations staff or other impartial party,

(b) keep the criteria for awards broad, and

(c) make sure your administrative procedures are fair and well monitored.

3. Choosing the right award program

The type of award program that will be most helpful to the company, whether different levels of awards should be included, and who should be eligible to participate needs to be decided before a successful program can be established. Naturally, determining what type of program will best suit the interests of the company depends upon what behaviors and activities the company wishes to reward.

The Texas Power & Light Company has an award program that focuses on improving productivity. Adopting the theme of "Solving the Productivity Puzzle," Charles Turner, supervisor of the company's productivity programs, and his staff developed a colorful approach to recognizing outstanding employee efforts. They developed "atta boy"-style awards for managers who wanted to let their employees know their extra effort is appreciated. The awards consist of certificates with colorful illustrations and graphics symbolizing the thrust of the award. For instance, the "oh-possum award" pictures a Disney-like possum character hanging on to a tree branch, while the copy reads, "This Award Certifies that _____ was willing to go far out on a limb for an idea that was believed in."

Another award is called the "People Builder Award." This award is presented for "outstanding performance in the area of employee development."

According to Turner, "positive feedback is the most critical element in any change process if a program is to succeed. We're asking managers to assist the company in providing such feedback to their employees by presenting these awards when they are deserving. The feedback from employees who receive them has been most rewarding and new awards are being suggested from all areas of the company.

"Texas Power & Light Company has always been a very strong and high-ranking company," says Turner, "but today you have to work hard at maintaining that standard."

Another award, the "Cultivator Award" does just that by rewarding supervisors or managers whose employee is promoted to a higher position in the company. The promoted worker and the recipient's supervisor sign the document for presentation at the most appropriate time — preferably in the company of his or her peers.

"Management has been defined as the development of people," Turner says. "It is the manager who is repeatedly teaching and developing new workers who later move on. A manager's effectiveness can really be seen by the turnover in the people he works with. We think maybe if a manager receives five or six of these awards, perhaps then his efforts will be recognized by top management."

As illustrated by the Texas Power & Light example, rewards don't have to be elaborate to be effective. In fact, many of the most effective awards provided to employees are simple. Yet these awards are powerful in terms of their effect on employee morale and productivity.

How can you establish a good system for rewarding your employees? Following are some simple guidelines:

(a) Tie incentives to results. Make it quite obvious to employees what they need to do to be rewarded.

(b) Consider the needs and abilities of the entire staff, not just your top performers. Consider providing rewards to novices for their efforts to learn rather than their ability to produce.

(c) Ask for input and advice from your employees when determining rewards and guidelines for winners. Your employees will often set higher standards for themselves than you do and will appreciate the fact that you asked for their input.

(d) Make sure that top management is committed to the program.

(e) Make the program flexible and adapt it to special situations.

(f) Provide rewards that are consistent with the performance goals you set.

(g) Let your employees know what's in it for them.

(h) Avoid the temptation to reward poor performers by making exceptions.

4. Recognition

Recognition is a very effective and accessible way to motivate your employees. It is also a tool that you have at your immediate disposal. Here are some tips:

(a) Make yourself available to talk to your people. Your simply being there is very important to the people who work for you. If you say you have an "open-door policy," abide by it. Your undivided and sincere attention to your employees is extremely motivating.

81

(b) Encourage people to work *with* you, not for you. Teamwork is more than a buzzword: it's an important way to encourage employees to meet department and company objectives. To reword a familiar saying, when your employees feel that they are a part of the solution they won't be a part of the problem.

(c) Tell your employees in advance about changes that affect them. As we'll see in a later chapter, involvement is another essential key to motivation.

(d) Give credit when due. Be quick to compliment.

(e) Make sure each person knows what is expected and how he or she is doing. Employees need to know what behaviors will be rewarded and what behaviors will be criticized. Make your expectations clear. Be sure your employees understand what these expectations are and how they fit into the overall goals of the company.

Simple guidelines? Certainly. Recognition *is* simple. And, because it's so simple, it's often overlooked. Don't fall into the trap that keeps many supervisors from developing a motivated staff. Be sure that you:

- Recognize employee motivators and dismotivators

- Help employees set clear goals

- Provide motivational performance reviews

- Give negative feedback motivationally

- Give credit and praise for accomplishment

- Develop effective reward systems

Do these things consistently with your employees and, like the people in the beginning of this chapter...they'll be recognized too.

7
GIVING NEGATIVE FEEDBACK MOTIVATIONALLY

As difficult as it can be to give positive acknowledgement to employees, negative feedback can be several times more difficult. However, it is crucial that you know how to effectively provide negative feedback to your employees so they can learn and grow in their positions. If given no indication that their performance or behavior is not living up to your expectations, they can't possible be expected to improve their performance. Let's take a look at how negative feedback can be used as a factor in motivating employees.

We all want approval and acceptance. Each of us needs to feel appreciated and admired. Blaise Pascal said, "Vanity is so secure in the heart of man that everyone wants to be admired, even I who write this, and you who read this."

Unfortunately, our need for approval is not always met. From the time we are born we are examined and judged by those around us. Our birth weight and length is compared to that of our brothers and sisters or family acquaintances. Soon the race is on to find who will take the first step or say the first word. We may hear negative comments because we cry too much, sleep too much, spit up, refuse to be toilet trained, fight with our siblings and friends, are spoiled, shy, or precocious.

As we grow, we become so used to these comments that we become critics ourselves and bring home tales from school of our mean teachers and the selfish, weird, or stupid youngsters we go to school with.

Criticism is so common in our society that we actually pay others to offer their views on movies, books, art, food, etc. These people are, in turn, subjected to a great deal of criticism themselves, perhaps in keeping with a slightly modified version of the saying "those who can, do, those who can't, become critics." To quote Zeuxis (c. 400 B.C.), "Criticism comes easier than craftsmanship." But, criticism is *not* easy and most managers avoid negative confrontations with their errant employees.

Why? Because it's unpleasant. It can make a manager feel like a "bad guy." There's a possibility that the employee will strike back and create a scene. There's a chance that the employee's performance will decline even more.

In his book *How to Increase Employee Competence* (McGraw-Hill, 1984), Norman C. Hill writes "Rules and standards provide a sense of security for people in the workforce. They demonstrate a concern of supervisors for the welfare of everyone. When they are followed, cooperation results. When any employees are allowed to indiscriminately violate work rules, chaos results."

Walter Mahler and William Wrightnour studied the practices of 210 managers in a manufacturing company, a supermarket chain, and a public utility. The results showed that when managers spent a portion of their time counseling employees, the employees —

(a) felt more satisfied with their work,

(b) believed that their managers supervised them adequately, and

(c) reported that they liked the way their bosses motivated them.

Most employees *want* to do a good job. If you're remiss in letting them know when they're not doing a good job, they cannot possibly improve their performance.

a. THE COST TO THE ORGANIZATION

Unresolved disciplinary issues can have a negative impact on the organization in many ways.

There may be direct dollar costs. Incompetence may cause inefficiencies, may result in damage to company equipment, may contribute to the loss of customers or clients, or may result in costly errors. There may be productivity costs. Work bottlenecks may be created since most jobs interrelate with others. You, as supervisor, may find yourself having to spend more of your time on training, counseling, and disciplining this one employee while the rest of your job is put on hold.

There will almost certainly be morale problems, especially if you fail to take action. Other employees will quickly become irritated if someone in their workgroup is not "pulling his or her weight" and is, in effect, "getting away with it."

You will also more than likely have problems with upper management. In fact, if you allow incompetence to go unchecked, your own work record will be tarnished.

b. POSITIVE VS. NEGATIVE CRITICISM

Discipline is not necessarily a negative event. In fact, criticism can be either positive or negative. Positive criticism focuses on identifying causes of some unsatisfactory behavior and changing the behavior to help the employee improve. The supervisor asks the question, "How can we make this situation better?"

Negative criticism is a reaction to an unsatisfactory behavior which involves lashing out and placing blame. The supervisor asks the question, "What can I do to teach this employee a lesson?" The thought process is "punish first — then ask why."

Negative criticism results in defensive and emotional reactions by the subordinate. The employee feels attacked and, in the short term, his or her behavior will include withdrawal and avoidance. In the long term, the undesired behavior will usually recur. You've treated the symptom but not the problem.

In short, negative criticism is a short-term solution that —

(a) creates ill will,

(b) slows motivation and productivity,

(c) affects the use of positive discipline in the future, and

(d) doesn't yield the changes you want, even in the short term.

Remember, however, that while negative criticism should be used carefully, it does have its place. Even negative feedback provides recognition. The worst thing a manager can do is pretend a problem does not exist. Because criticism is difficult to give, many supervisors and managers often hesitate to approach workers whose performance is unsatisfactory. In their efforts to avoid unpleasant confrontations, they instead begin to ignore these workers. Unfortunately, unattended problems will not go away. Instead, they tend to accumulate and multiply. The performance of an employee who is getting no recognition at all is unlikely to improve.

By taking early, effective, and — preferably — positive steps to employee discipline, you can head off a major problem before it develops.

c. WHY WE DECIDE NOT TO CRITICIZE

There are many reasons we choose not to express criticism. We may be afraid of offending the other person and hurting our relationship. We may be afraid of starting a full-blown argument. We may not want to seem petty or unreasonable. Other common excuses for saying nothing include the following:

- He or she will no longer like me.

- "If you can't say something nice, say nothing."
- People cannot take criticism.

Let's examine these excuses.

1. He or she will no longer like me

Being a supervisor or manager is not a popularity contest. Of course, you would rather have employees like you than dislike you. What you really need as a supervisor, though, is respect — and motivated employees. You get neither if you fail to provide timely and valid criticism.

2. "If you can't say something nice, say nothing"

It's possible that your parents told you this when you were quite young and your interpersonal contacts were limited to the playground. As a supervisor, however, this rule is not sensible. Following it could result in never speaking to some employees!

3. People cannot take criticism

People need criticism — especially if those people happen to be your employees. Without criticism, you cannot expect your employees to improve their behavior, their performance, or their motivation. What this statement really means is, "People cannot take unfounded criticism."

d. WHY EMPLOYEES BECOME PROBLEMS

Habits that require disciplinary action don't develop overnight. In most cases, the supervisor should have been able to spot early warning signs well in advance of the need for desperate action. Spotting a problem at an early stage allows the opportunity for positive counseling and intervention before a major crisis develops.

Be alert to a potential problem arising if —

- there has been a decline in performance,
- the employee appears to be apathetic or withdrawn,

- the employee is a "whiner," continually complaining about very trivial aspects of the job,

- you have found it difficult to establish a good working relationship with the employee,

- the employee is reluctant or refuses to discuss the problem,

- the employee has continuing interpersonal problems with others in the organization,

- the employee resents criticism, or

- the employee's behavior is beginning to negatively affect others in the work group.

After these initial warning signals, the problem typically becomes more serious. At this stage you will be faced with some very common causes for discipline: absence without leave, disobedience, insubordination, or non-performance of job duties. When an employee problem has reached this stage it's a sign that you've waited too long to take action.

e. BEFORE TAKING DISCIPLINARY ACTION

Once a problem has been identified, it's time for you to take action. But before you do, there are several questions that you will need to ask yourself:

(a) Did the employee know and understand the rule that was broken or the procedure that was not followed?

(b) Was the employee warned of possible disciplinary consequences?

(c) Is the rule or procedure that was violated necessary for the orderly, efficient, and safe operation of the business?

(d) Was a fair and objective investigation conducted to determine whether the employee actually violated the rule?

(e) Has the company applied rules, procedures, and penalties fairly and consistently to all employees?

You must determine all the facts before having a discussion with the errant employee. If you don't, you may find that your decision to discipline was incorrect and you have alienated the employee.

Let's assume that you have a problem employee who, it has been reported, is consistently coming in late and has been intimidating other employees into covering up for this tardiness. Before you confront the employee you may need to consult —

(a) the person(s) making the report,

(b) other employees,

(c) your immediate supervisor, and

(d) the human resources department.

You will want to gather all of the facts and to be as specific as possible in terms of:

- What happened?
- When did it happen?
- How often did it happen?
- Who knew it happened?

You will want to review this employee's past history to determine length of service, specifics of past performance, and the possibility of other disciplinary actions.

You will want to compare this situation with other similar situations that have occurred at your company. What have other supervisors done with employees who have exhibited the same or a similar problem? What have you done in similar situations?

You will want to know:

- Who was involved in the incident?

- What led up to the incident?

- What feelings were expressed by those involved?

After you have gathered all the facts, you will want to analyze the situation to determine:

- How the involved parties (and you) may have contributed to the problem.

- How the involved parties (and you) can contribute to a solution.

- Whether there are differing perceptions and misunderstandings contributing to the problem.

- To what extent outside forces influenced the problem.

- The probability that a meaningful improvement can be obtained in the near future.

f. EXERCISING POSITIVE DISCIPLINE

Douglas McGregor formulated what he called the "hot stove rule" as the basis for implementing positive discipline. His theory is that effective discipline is analogous to touching a hot stove. When you touch a stove, the consequences are immediate, impersonal, predictable, and consistent. When your hand is burned you know *immediately* that you have done something wrong. The fact that you were burned is a function of the stove — it is not a function of who you are or of any aspect of your personality. The consequence was, therefore, *impersonal.* Every time you touch the stove you will be burned — the consequence is *predictable.* The same thing would happen to anyone who touched the stove regardless of their age, sex, attitudes, etc. The consequence of being burned is *consistent.*

Effective discipline incorporates the same principles: immediacy, predictability, impersonality, and consistency.

1. Immediacy

When discipline is necessary, you should approach the employee as soon as possible after the violation has been noticed or reported. At this point, the incident will be fresh in both your mind and the employee's mind. If you wait too long, the impact of your confrontation will be lessened.

You should, however, time your confrontation so that you approach the employee at the optimum time. For instance, you don't want to corner the employee the minute he or she comes to work on Monday morning or just as he or she is leaving on a Friday afternoon.

When you do approach the employee, you should state immediately, in as few words as possible, just what it is that's causing you concern and let the employee know that a rule or order has been violated.

2. Predictability

The employee should be well aware that the behavior he or she exhibited was in violation of some company rule or previous order. It should be very clear that *anyone* exhibiting that behavior would be disciplined.

You should have been very clear in the past about what behavior you will and will not tolerate and what standards of performance you expect from people in your department.

In dealing with a subsequent infraction, then, the employee will be well aware that he or she has violated a rule or previous order and will not be surprised by the action you take.

3. Impersonality

Employees sometimes feel as though their supervisor is out to get them. It's important that your employees know that when they are disciplined it is because of what they did and not who they are. You should be just as willing to approach

91

one of your star performers with a performance issue as you are one of your "problem" employees.

When practicing positive discipline, it is important that you do not treat your employee as an adversary and that you address the issue civilly without lecturing, nagging, or losing your temper.

Let the employee tell his or her side of the story. Ask questions only to obtain details. Listen with an open mind and give the employee the benefit of the doubt.

4. Consistency

It is extremely important that you and the company you work for are consistent in your discipline of employees. Discipline must be consistent within your department *and* throughout the company.

To determine the appropriate course of action to take, you should find out how other employees were treated in similar circumstances. Talk to other supervisors, the personnel or human resources manager, or others knowledgeable about company policy and precedent.

Both because you want employees to be treated fairly and because you want to avoid legal liability, you should make every possible effort to ensure that your disciplinary actions are consistent.

g. THE DISCIPLINARY CONFERENCE

When you meet with an employee who needs to be disciplined there are several things you must keep in mind and several steps you should have already taken. As we've seen previously, you should have gathered as many facts as possible about the situation. And you should have reviewed the employee's personnel file to determine if this behavior has occurred previously. In addition, you should make sure that the employee is well aware of the reason for this meeting.

When you meet you should:

(a) Have notes and make use of them.

(b) Explain the facts you have gathered as fully as possible.

(c) Ask the employee to give his/her perspective. Allow the opportunity for some emotional venting.

(d) Discuss the situation in depth with the employee and explore various ways the situation might have been handled differently.

(e) Make a determination, in your own mind, as to whether discipline is justified.

(f) Explain what you intend to do and why — refer to company policy and precedent. Try to obtain the employee's agreement that he or she has done something wrong and that discipline is necessary.

(g) Be very specific about what the consequence will be for continued infractions.

(h) Provide a system for follow-up. Be specific about how future behavior will be monitored, what results you expect, and how you expect the employee (with your help) to obtain them.

Here are some additional guidelines for assuring positive discipline:

- Give fair warning. Let the employee know that "Your behavior is inappropriate."

- Listen to the employee's side until you fully understand the motivation for the behavior.

- Deal with the objective issues and not your own subjective emotions and feelings. Say "When you're late, you create additional work for others in the department" not "You're totally irresponsible and you make me look like a poor manager when you come in late every day."

- Discipline privately. Make every possible effort to avoid embarrassing the employee in front of others.

- Be sure to find out how the employee feels about the action you are taking. Does he or she feel that you are being fair?

- Be sure to obtain the employee's commitment to improve.

- Document the incident in writing and include it in the employee's personnel file.

8
EMPLOYEE INVOLVEMENT

Pitney Bowes Inc. has a Council of Personnel Relations which includes managers and employees elected by their peers. Employees meet with their elected representatives and a supervisor bi-weekly. Any problems not solved at this level go to the department council, then to the division council, then to the management council. At each step, employees elected by their peers serve as representatives. That's involvement.

Employee task forces at Digital Equipment Corporation, 3M, Emerson Electric, Exxon, and others resolve issues ranging from the simple to the complex. That's involvement.

The average Toyota employee offers 18 ideas to management per year and 90% of these suggestions are put to use. What does this mean to the company? In just one year, 500,000 suggestions were received — suggestions that saved the company $230 million. That's involvement.

Employee involvement means involving company representatives at every level of the company. Employees are involved in decisions that can be as basic as whether to charge employees for coffee or as far-reaching as whether to start an employee stock ownership plan.

Employee involvement allows a company to share decision making. Employees become directly responsible for the work they do.

A 1987 study conducted by the University of Manitoba in Winnipeg concluded that most employees expressed greater job satisfaction in a participatory decision-making environment. The study concluded that managers should share their decision-making power in the interests of individual employees, the overall organization, and themselves.

Today's corporate leaders know the importance of employee involvement and how it can affect profits. Employees can be a company's most valuable resource. As more companies come to realize just how valuable, they are increasing involvement.

The changing workforce also contributes to the need for employee involvement. Putting it simply, employees are demanding to be involved. In *The Gold Collar Worker*, Robert E. Kelley writes, "Gold collar workers expect to participate in decisions that affect them and their work. Over 84% of college graduates, in fact, indicate that they will be more satisfied, and therefore more productive, if they are allowed active participation. Because they consider themselves adults, they resent and bristle against the traditional parent-child relationship fostered by most old-line organizations. Rather than trusting that management knows best, they insist on adult transactions based on competence, respect, and the satisfaction of mutual needs."

In the late 1970s, the National Science Foundation noted several factors that influenced productivity. They were autonomy, access to job-related information, a less rigid structure, and a variety of tasks. All of these things lead to involvement.

A public agenda report authored by Daniel Yankelovich and John Immerwahn indicates that employees want to do their best but are often discouraged by management. They suggest that management give workers a financial stake in their organizations. They also suggest flattening the management hierarchy. They feel, "Many organizations that have been successful at winning high levels of commitment are characterized by relatively flat organizational charts and by status differences that are not invidious: they do not shout the message, 'managers are a class apart.'"

What can you do to give your employees the involvement they need? We'll take a look at several possibilities ranging from the simple to the complex.

a. THE CORPORATE ADVANTAGE

Employee involvement was first used to keep employees happy. As workers became more demanding, management felt a strong push to provide better working conditions, better benefits, and more involvement in decisions.

What a surprise to discover that once these employees became involved, strange things began to happen. Motivation increased. Productivity increased. There were more new ideas. Innovative techniques, processes, and products were introduced. And, ultimately, the bottom line was fattened.

Something that was started to keep employees satisfied led to a direct, positive impact on company profits.

b. DECISION MAKING — MORE THAN A MANAGERIAL PREROGATIVE

The change in managerial attitude has, perhaps, paralleled the change in parental attitude. Today's parents are allowing their children a more equal role in family decisions: today's corporations are allowing employees a more equal role in corporate decisions.

Managers are realizing, and rightly so, that employees are more likely to participate in an activity that they are committed to. They are more likely to be committed if they are involved in the decision making behind the development of the activity.

In *The Gold Collar Worker*, Kelley writes, "Gold collar workers want access to relevant information, consultation, and true participation in management decision making. Before committing themselves to implementation, they require active involvement in formulation. Taking orders, particularly orders they perceive as illogical, insults their intelligence and often results in a creative shutdown."

There are two very important reasons that managers should strive for employee participation in decision making.

1. Reduced resentment over "taking orders"

As we've already implied, employees don't like being pushed around. If employees are given orders and allowed no input, you will see lowered morale, poor attitude, and increased turnover. Employees should be involved because...

2. They know more than you do

When it comes to the day-to-day operation of your company or department, nobody knows better what will work than the job holder. Nobody can offer better information on changes to procedures, policies, or operations than the person who does the job, day after day, week after week, and month after month.

If you don't gather input from these people, you are likely to be hurting yourself and your company. Consider the following example.

Jackie was the personnel director of a small consulting company. As the company grew, departments developed and employees were divided by specialty: planning, promotion, production, etc. The clerical staff, however, remained a separate group — bull-pen style.

Jackie found that evaluating these employees was becoming very difficult. Each clerical person worked with one or two middle-management people. However, daily work assignments were given by a service coordinator who was also responsible for semi-annual reviews. Jackie felt that this did not allow for valuable input from the middle-management people.

Jackie, with permission from upper management, decided to assign clerical people to specific departments. This is what happened:

(a) Because clerical workers were now located throughout the company, they felt isolated from each other.

(b) More clerical workers were hired in some departments. In other departments, clerical workers often had nothing to do. There was no longer a central service coordinator to monitor and distribute assignments.

(c) Morale suffered. In individual departments, clerical workers began to feel as though they were at the bottom of the totem pole.

What went wrong here?

Putting it quite simply, Jackie failed to involve the people involved. While she consulted with management, she didn't seek input from the clerical workers or from their service coordinator.

If she had, she would have learned about possible problems. The big error: not involving the involved.

Is it necessary to involve employees in *all* decisions made? It is if they're affected by the decision. We all accept orders more easily if we've offered our own opinions and suggestions before a decision is made. You may not use every comment or suggestion an employee makes. However, by involving your employees you will have more information for decision making. You'll increase your chance of making a decision that has a positive effect on motivation and productivity.

c. MEETINGS — A PROBLEM FOR "PRODUCTIVE" MANAGERS

At 8:30 a.m. you come into the office and check your mail. On top of a heaping pile of correspondence, journals, and miscellaneous urgent materials, is a memo — a memo which informs you of a meeting to be held at 1:00 p.m.

"Oh no!" you groan, "Not another meeting."

You, like many other businesspeople, are so concerned about getting out of meetings that you've forgotten what you could be getting out of meetings.

Statistics in the *AMA Review*, a publication of the American Management Association, show that managers spend up to 53% of their time in meetings. The biggest complaints about these meetings are that they are late getting started, not well organized, and too long. Yet meetings, when handled properly, can serve some very useful purposes.

Meetings are especially useful when designed to encourage involvement of employees at every level of the organization. Do you have regular meetings with employees to let them know about company activities and to ask for their participation in decisions?

Many companies have a regular staff meeting. This is usually not enough to gain the level of involvement you're looking for. With a small company (10 employees or less) it may well work. As the number of employees in your company increases, however, you'll find a greater need for regular meetings at many levels. Some variations might be:

- Individual department meetings

- Department head meetings within a division

- Managerial meetings involving only top management

- Supervisory meetings involving middle management

- Production meetings involving employees who are producing a product or service

- One-on-one meetings within departments between managers and individual employees

- Meetings between two departments that work very closely together

As you can probably already see, the possibilities are endless.

How do you decide when meetings are necessary? As we saw in chapter 5, communication is vital in employee motivation. Meetings are an important way to increase communication and encourage employee involvement.

Do meetings waste time? Sometimes.

So, before you start company-wide meetings between every possible level and combination of employee, consider the following two questions:

1. What is the purpose of the meeting? Is it ensuring that everyone receives accurate and equal information? Gathering contributions for decision making? Building a team to carry out decisions?

2. Who should be included in the meeting? Ask yourself who must attend the meeting. Choose meeting participants based on what they can contribute or what they will get out of the meeting. Then consider what might be the best number of meeting participants. Here is a general guide:

- Problem solving meetings — 5 or less

- Problem identifying meetings — 10 or less

- Reviews or presentations — 30 or less

- Motivational — as many as possible

Make sure the people you select for participation in the meeting have the ability to make decisions, the responsibility for carrying out any decisions made, the information you need to make decisions, and a need to know about the decisions made.

Meetings can be a company's biggest waste of productive time. When planned and run properly, however, meetings can save time.

d. ATTITUDE SURVEYS

"I wonder what they think about...?"

How many times have you or other managers in your company wondered what your employees think? The best way to discover what your employees think is to ask them. Asking each employee individually, however, can be time consuming and inefficient. Managers should constantly seek input from employees. However, when you want an overall measure of employee feeling on particular issues, you need an attitude survey.

Attitude surveys can measure employees' feelings on their jobs, their supervisors, their coworkers, company benefits, overall management, and the quality of products and services produced.

There are two important things you must consider before doing an employee attitude survey. You and the company must be prepared to —

(a) report the results of the survey to employees, and

(b) take action based on the results of the surveys.

If you are unwilling to follow either of these two guidelines, there is no point in conducting an attitude survey.

Company morale will be improved by listening to and acting on employee suggestions. If you are going to the trouble of conducting an employee attitude survey, you must be prepared to act on the comments and suggestions you receive.

102

You could use Worksheet #3 to survey the attitudes of employees in your company.

Attitude surveys are valuable for monitoring the feelings of employees. Whether you design a survey specifically for your company or use a standardized survey, the information you receive will provide you with the following:

(a) A measure of what strengths and weaknesses employees feel the company has

(b) A measure of how effective management is at managing

(c) An opportunity for encouraging employee communication of thoughts, feelings, concerns, suggestions, and complaints

(d) A yardstick against which to compare previous and future survey results to determine whether the company is improving

(e) An opportunity for unhappy employees to "let management have it"

A company's planning function can't be completed without regular input from its employees. Attitude surveys provide you with the input you need.

e. QUALITY CIRCLES

1. What is a quality circle?

Employees are no longer working for money alone. Today's workers are also concerned with social needs and self-worth. A study of 175,000 workers in 159 North American companies showed that most believed they were not respected as individuals. They also felt their jobs lacked challenge and satisfaction. Salary levels were not a source of discontent.

There are five qualities of Japanese management practice that can be used with these employees.

(a) A longer-term view to business practice

(b) A partnership in the needs of firm and employee

(c) Openness in organizational structure and interactive communication

(d) Sharing of organizational power

(e) A search for improving productivity

The Japanese place a strong emphasis on communication. Japanese managers also emphasize employee involvement. They demand more responsible participation of all workers and believe that all employees are capable of thinking a problem through.

Quality circles are a technique of management that started in Japan. In the early 1960s, Kaoru Ishikawa, president of Musashi Institute of Technology in Tokyo, worked closely with the Japanese Union of Scientists and Engineers to organize the first quality circles in Japan.

Typically, a circle consists of a group of 5 to 15 people who work together in a company or plant. They meet together on a voluntary basis once or twice a week to identify and solve problems. Their specific purpose is to make their work team more productive.

There are several important principles in the quality circle concept:

(a) The employee is expert

(b) The employee wants to contribute

(c) Participation in the group is voluntary

(d) The circle members choose the problems they will deal with

(e) Outside help from consultants or management is available if needed and requested

(f) Suggestions do not have to be implemented by management

WORKSHEET #3
QUALITY OF WORK LIFE SURVEY

Questions 1 to 43 use the following scale:

FREQUENCY SCALE: % of time

1 = Almost never (0% to 10% of the time)

2 = Rarely (11% to 30% of the time)

3 = Occasionally (31% to 50% of the time)

4 = Frequently (51% to 70% of the time)

5 = Very frequently (71% to 90% of the time)

6 = Almost always (over 90% of the time)

1. My boss is willing to help me improve my skills so I can do a better job.   1   2   3   4   5   6

2. I know the role that I play in achieving company goals.   1   2   3   4   5   6

3. My department operates as a team.   1   2   3   4   5   6

4. My boss encourages me to be creative in my work.   1   2   3   4   5   6

5. My talents and training are being utilized in my job.   1   2   3   4   5   6

6. I have the opportunity to make a contribution to the success of this company.   1   2   3   4   5   6

7. The pace at which I need to work to get my job done is reasonable.   1   2   3   4   5   6

8. The regular staff meetings are informative.   1   2   3   4   5   6

9. The suggestion box works well for getting new ideas fairly evaluated.   1   2   3   4   5   6

10. I am encouraged by my boss to share my ideas on how to improve our company.

    1 2 3 4 5 6

11. I have confidence in upper management to make good decisions for the company.

    1 2 3 4 5 6

12. We share information with each other in order to help each other do our jobs. 1 2 3 4 5 6

13. Management acts as if they want me to stay with the company.

    1 2 3 4 5 6

14. Company policies and procedures are applied consistently throughout the company.

    1 2 3 4 5 6

15. There is a real sense of teamwork and cooperation within my department. 1 2 3 4 5 6

16. My job is interesting. 1 2 3 4 5 6

17. I plan on working at this company indefinitely.

    1 2 3 4 5 6

18. This company employs enough people to operate productively. 1 2 3 4 5 6

19. The company has helped me to learn about other departments and their responsibilities.

    1 2 3 4 5 6

20. I believe employees are being totally honest on the attitudes surveys of their boss.

    1 2 3 4 5 6

21. My ideas and suggestions will get a fair hearing from my boss. 1 2 3 4 5 6

22. I have access to the information I need to get my job done.   1   2   3   4   5   6

23. I am aware of our goals for the company this year.   1   2   3   4   5   6

24. Input from associates is asked for when management is considering changes in company policies and procedures.   1   2   3   4   5   6

25. My job is challenging.   1   2   3   4   5   6

26. The demands placed on me by other departments to get my job done are reasonable.   1   2   3   4   5   6

27. The company newsletter is a valuable communication tool.   1   2   3   4   5   6

28. Upper management listens to what the staff advisory council has to say.   1   2   3   4   5   6

29. I am comfortable with my job security.   1   2   3   4   5   6

30. Upper management keeps us informed about important developments affecting the company as a whole.   1   2   3   4   5   6

31. Associate input is used by management when considering changes in company policy and procedures.   1   2   3   4   5   6

32. Teamwork and cooperation is encouraged by my director.   1   2   3   4   5   6

33. All things considered, this is a good place to work.   1   2   3   4   5   6

34. The demands placed on me by my manager to get my job done are reasonable.

    1   2   3   4   5   6

35. I make a point of reading postings on the bulletin board.

    1   2   3   4   5   6

36. My boss has confidence in me to do a good job.

    1   2   3   4   5   6

37. I am comfortable with my job stability.

    1   2   3   4   5   6

38. Teamwork and cooperation is encouraged by my director.

    1   2   3   4   5   6

39. I get a sense of accomplishment from my job.

    1   2   3   4   5   6

40. When I finish a day's work, I feel as though I have done something worthwhile.

    1   2   3   4   5   6

41. The amount of overtime I have to work to get my job done is reasonable.

    1   2   3   4   5   6

42. I feel free to ask for information I need to get my job done.

    1   2   3   4   5   6

43. The notice given when overtime is needed is reasonable.

    1   2   3   4   5   6

Questions 44 to 95 use the following scale:

AGREE - DISAGREE SCALE:

1 = Strongly disagree (or dissatisfied)

2 = Usually disagree (or dissatisfied)

3 = Somewhat disagree (or dissatisfied)

4 = Somewhat agree (or satisfied)

5 = Usually agree (or satisfied)

6 = Strongly agree (or satisfied)

44. Upper management takes the best interests of our employees into consideration in corporate decision making. 1 2 3 4 5 6

45. I am important to the success of this company. 1 2 3 4 5 6

46. The personnel handbook contains valuable information on company policies and procedures. 1 2 3 4 5 6

47. I feel that I am part of my department team. 1 2 3 4 5 6

48. Employees are treated fairly in this company. 1 2 3 4 5 6

49. My coworkers within my department are trustworthy. 1 2 3 4 5 6

50. The people I regularly work with in other departments are trustworthy. 1 2 3 4 5 6

51. I am fairly compensated for the work I do. 1 2 3 4 5 6

52. I have a good understanding of our insurance benefits. 1 2 3 4 5 6

53. I have had adequate on-the-job training to perform according to company standards. 1 2 3 4 5 6

54. I am proud to work for this company. 1 2 3 4 5 6

55. I like my job.   1   2   3   4   5   6

56. Surveys like this are an effective way to let upper management know how employees feel .
                          1   2   3   4   5   6

57. Management will make constructive use of this survey.   1   2   3   4   5   6

58. I can tell my boss about my work concerns and problems without fear of reprisal.
                          1   2   3   4   5   6

59. Upper management's goals for our company are realistic.   1   2   3   4   5   6

60. Changes in company policies and procedures are communicated clearly to me by my boss.
                          1   2   3   4   5   6

61. I feel that I am part of the company team.
                          1   2   3   4   5   6

62. I don't have to compromise my personal ethical standards to work here.   1   2   3   4   5   6

63. I have good working relationships with coworkers in my department.   1   2   3   4   5   6

64. I have good working relationships with people outside my department.   1   2   3   4   5   6

65. I understand how our compensation system works.   1   2   3   4   5   6

66. The benefits we have meet my needs.
                          1   2   3   4   5   6

67. I'm encouraged to improve my performance through additional training and education.
    1   2   3   4   5   6

68. I would recommend this company to my friends as a good place to work.   1   2   3   4   5   6

69. I know how to get my job description updated.
    1   2   3   4   5   6

70. I can trust my boss to keep confidential information confidential.   1   2   3   4   5   6

71. Our department cooperates well with the other departments we work with.   1   2   3   4   5   6

72. Upper management is honest in dealing with associates.   1   2   3   4   5   6

73. The coworkers in my department are able to perform their jobs competently. 1   2   3   4   5   6

74. My coworkers in other departments are able to perform their jobs competently.
    1   2   3   4   5   6

75. The pay for my position is fair based on what other organizations in the area are paying for similar positions.   1   2   3   4   5   6

76. Company benefits are explained clearly in the handbook.   1   2   3   4   5   6

77. I am respected by my coworkers for my ability to do my job.   1   2   3   4   5   6

78. The company's health insurance program is a good benefit.   1   2   3   4   5   6

79. My boss trusts me to keep confidential information confidential. 1 2 3 4 5 6

80. Changes in company policies and procedures are communicated in a timely manner.
    1 2 3 4 5 6

81. We have a positive, upbeat attitude about doing business. 1 2 3 4 5 6

82. People in my department treat me with respect.
    1 2 3 4 5 6

83. The people I work with in other departments on a regular basis treat me with respect.
    1 2 3 4 5 6

84. Merit pay increases are administered consistently.
    1 2 3 4 5 6

85. I know how to get answers to my questions on benefits. 1 2 3 4 5 6

86. I get positive reinforcement from my boss when I do a good job. 1 2 3 4 5 6

87. I think this company should get more involved in promoting health and wellness for employees.
    1 2 3 4 5 6

88. I have seen improvement in teamwork and cooperation between departments over the last year.
    1 2 3 4 5 6

89. I get the cooperation I need from the others in my department to do my job well.
    1 2 3 4 5 6

90. I get the cooperation I need from other departments in order to do my job.

     1   2   3   4   5   6

91. My pay increases are based on how well I do my
job.   1   2   3   4   5   6

92. My performance reviews help me learn how to improve my job performance. 1   2   3   4   5   6

93. A survey would be a good way for employees to
help improve their boss's performance.

     1   2   3   4   5   6

94. Our job evaluation process has helped us to be
more consistent in determining what we pay for
each job.   1   2   3   4   5   6

95. The company retirement plan is a good benefit to
have.   1   2   3   4   5   6

96. I would prefer that my performance appraisal be
conducted in a room other than my boss's office.
❑ yes ❑ no ❑ doesn't matter

97. List up to five things you like most about working
for this company.

_____

_____

_____

_____

_____

_____

_____

_____

98. List up to five things you like least about working for this company.

_____

_____

_____

_____

_____

_____

_____

99. Are there questions that were not included in this survey that should be on it in the future?

_____

_____

_____

_____

_____

100. Please use this space to make any additional comments or to refer to specific questions on the survey.

_____

_____

_____

_____

_____

_____

_____

_____

_____

PLEASE READ!

These questions are designed to help us better analyze the results of this survey. How long you have been here, whether or not you are in management, and what department you are in will give us valuable insight into how we are operating. Members of departments with less than five employees (including manager) may choose not to identify themselves in the results in order to protect confidentiality.

1. I belong to the following department:

❏ Finance
❏ Printing
❏ Bulk mail
❏ Ship/rec. & A/V
❏ Editorial
❏ Program dev.
❏ Program services
❏ Customer relations
❏ Advertising
❏ Support services
❏ Management information services
❏ Directors and their assistants

2. I am:

❏ Associate
❏ Management (includes directors, managers, senior planners)

3. Length of employment:

❏ Under 1 year   ❏ 1 to 2 years
❏ over 5 years   ❏ 3 to 5 years

2. How quality circles work

The quality circle process is relatively simple. It consists of problem identification, data gathering, brainstorming, and cause and effect analysis. Eventually, the circle gives management a proposal for dealing with the problems that were identified.

The steps are also quite simple:

(a) Determine the problem to be attacked

(b) Select a specific part of the problem for detailed investigation and analysis

(c) Gather and analyze data related to the problem to determine possible and actual causes

(d) Determine a specific course of action to solve the problem

(e) Develop a plan and timetable for initiating these actions

(f) Present management with the proposed plan and timetable

(g) Implement the plan

(h) Follow up to determine the effectiveness of the course of action taken

(i) Communicate the results to top management

(j) Focus on a new problem and repeat the process

An important part of the quality circle process is brainstorming. Brainstorming sessions are intended to generate a large number of ideas. During these sessions, several principles should be followed:

- Encourage free thought

- Do not allow criticism of any ideas presented

- Ensure that all members of the circle have an equal opportunity to participate in the brainstorming

- Write down all ideas generated

It is easy to see the role of involvement in quality circles. Quality circles include people with hands-on knowledge of the company. Circle members have the information they need for effective problem solving.

3. Quality circles in North America

The first U.S. quality circles were established at Smith Kline Instruments of Palo Alto, California in the fall of 1970. Later, in 1973, Wayne Rieker, Operations Manager at Lockheed's Missile and Space Division in Sunnyvale, California, visited several Japanese plants that were using the quality circle concept. When he returned to the United States, he made several innovations to the quality circle concept. He —

(a) suggested a training period for everyone involved in quality circles before launching a quality circle movement,

(b) developed the role of facilitator — a person to act as a training expert or program manager,

(c) scheduled meetings to take place on company time,

(d) developed a structured sequence of problem identification, data gathering, and analysis of cause and effect, and

(e) suggested that members of the circle present their findings *as a group* to management.

The concept has caught on well in the United States. Today, more than 500 companies make use of quality circles. These companies include Allstate, Honeywell, Lockheed, General Dynamics and Westinghouse. Honeywell has more than 9000 quality teams.

4. Do quality circles work?

The Quality Control Circle is designed to:

(a) Help improve and develop company activities

117

(b) Build a happy workplace

(c) Take advantage of all of an employee's capabilities

Circle activities are designed to increase morale. The theory is that a company can realize full employee potential only by investing in their training and giving them the power to influence decisions.

In the November 4, 1981, issue of the *Quality Circles Journal*, Dr. Ishikawa was quoted as saying, "As enterprises exist in human society, the main aim of management is to respect humanity and build a worthwhile, lively, happy and bright workshop that can display human capabilities fully and draw out infinite possibilities of the people related to their enterprises (customers, workers and their families, stockholders and circulation). The idea of profit first is an old-style selfish concept."

Do quality circles work? Reports suggest that they do. In *The Productivity Challenge*, Michael LeBoeuf cites the following results:

(a) A quality circle of line operators at Texas Instruments increased output of an assembly-line operator from 10,000 to 18,500 units per day. As a result, the company saved $1.2 million annually.

(b) A circle of clerical workers in a corporate mailroom reduced misdirected mail by 50% and saved the company $62,000 per year.

(c) A circle of skilled machinists was losing time locating precision tools. They studied the problem and solved it by building a portable tool cart with space for the appropriate tools. The cart could be quickly moved and the spaces were designed to that tools could be rapidly removed and replaced without misplacement. Estimated annual savings were $157,000.

(d) By studying the causes of failing solenoids, a circle of Japanese operators at an auto parts plant reduced the failure rate from 7% to 1% in a nine-month period.

(e) A circle of typists in an insurance company studied the problem of typists' errors. The problem was attributed to poor knowledge of terminology and errors were reduced by scheduling an hour of training each week on title policy and procedures.

(f) Employee suggestions from quality circles in a large manufacturing company saved the company $750,000 the first year by providing ideas for reducing scrap materials.

In the September, 1981, issue of Hewlett-Packard's in-house publication, *Measure*, a quality circle leader stated, "One of the benefits of quality teams that I have seen is individual, personal growth. Employees who were very, very quiet people have been willing to make phone calls to support the group and to talk to engineers. They've all learned how to relate to each other, how to listen and how to compromise. They've also learned how to collect data, write minutes and do public speaking — everyone on the team had a part in our first presentation. Amazing things happened in our group."

Robert Ostlund, an industrial engineer, is just as pleased with Honeywell's experience. "The short-term productivity benefits are a nice bonus, but one shouldn't confuse these good results with the real goal. Teams are a long-term commitment to a change in management style, not a short-term program. We certainly are encouraged by the short-term productivity gains because solving production problems is one of the goals. But improving employee attitudes and developing employee skills and potential are equally important."

Can anything go wrong with the quality circle concept? Yes, actually, there are a few potential problem areas:

(a) Resistance by middle managers or supervisors

(b) Poor training of quality circle leaders and/or members

(c) Consistent failure by management to implement quality circle proposals

(d) Failure to monitor results of the quality circle process

(e) Establishing quality circles that deviate from the basic structure that has been developed successfully for hundreds of other companies

With quality circles (or any type of employee involvement device) the motto should be "listen and listen well." Allow for and encourage involvement from all employees for problem identification and resolution.

Sincere, company-wide commitment to the quality circle process is a sound guarantee for success.

f. MBO — MANAGING BY OBJECTIVES...FOR INVOLVEMENT

Another management "standard" of the 1970s and 1980s that is waning in popularity is MBO or Management by Objectives. However, as we will see, it is not that these techniques aren't applicable. It's just that the MBO principles have become so much a part of the everyday operating systems of so many companies that the buzzword itself is not so commonly used.

1. What is Management by Objectives?

Peter Drucker coined the term "management by objectives" in 1954. Since that time it has become confused and misdefined. In the words of Walter S. Wikstrom, "management by objectives has become an all-purpose term, meaning almost anything one chooses to have it mean."

Dale McConkey, associate professor of management at the University of Wisconsin — Madison, has noted that data is difficult to obtain on the number of organizations using MBO because of the "uncertainty concerning what MBO is."

As defined by Peter Drucker, MBO is "a principle of management that will give full scope to individual strength and responsibility and at the same time give common direction of vision and effort, establish teamwork, and harmonize the goals of the individual with the common weal."

Management by Objectives uses company objectives to provide a basis for managing the organization. The focus is on goal setting with an emphasis on employee involvement. Employees help to set goals and specific objectives for reaching the goals. MBO is more than a planning and control system: it's also a very powerful change agent for organizational development.

Employee participation provides the structure for the MBO principle. In short, what MBO manages to accomplish for an organization is teamwork. Upper and middle management work together with subordinates. They establish goals that meet the objectives of the organization and suit the needs of the employees.

2. How MBO works

Implementation is the most critical stage in an MBO program. As part of this stage, it's necessary to decide on a method of implementation. There are three possibilities: one level at a time, one department only, or all levels at once.

The one-level-at-a-time approach works well in large companies with many managers and many levels of management. Smaller companies may be effective at introducing MBO to the entire company at once. Companies that are not sure they want to launch a full-scale MBO program can test one department first. This avoids the investment of a great deal of time and resources on something that may not prove viable.

The steps in implementation are the same regardless of the method used. They are:

(a) Hold an initial meeting for all members of the company. Provide an overview of the MBO program and an outline of how implementation will proceed.

(b) Provide orientation training seminars to present the philosophy of the program to secure enthusiastic commitment. The orientation session is usually presented first to management. Management then introduces the program to others, one level at a time.

(c) Present top management objectives to lower levels of the company so goals can be established.

(d) Evaluate performance based on the accomplishment of these goals.

(e) Develop a system of weekly meetings involving all employees. At these meetings, discuss any problems that may have developed, provide clarification, or revise objectives that are unsatisfactory in any way.

(f) Encourage employees to express their opinions at any time. Make special efforts to keep communication channels open.

There are five essential elements in any MBO plan:

1. Firm assignment of responsibility for taking an action

2. The timing of each step

3. Identification of additional resources needed

4. The estimated dollar costs of each major step

5. An estimate of the benefits expected

3. Making MBO work

MBO programs, like quality circles, aren't always successful. We saw evidence of this in the opening paragraph of this section. A primary problem with MBO today is that everyone has their own idea of how to develop a program and how it should work. Varying from the pure form of MBO as established by Peter Drucker and refined by Dale McConkey is just one way to develop a program that doesn't work. There are others.

In the October, 1972, issue of *Management Review* an American Management Association Publication, Dale McConkey listed "20 Ways to Kill MBO" They are:

1. Consider MBO a panacea
2. Tell 'em their objectives
3. Leave out staff managers
4. Delegate executive direction
5. Create a paper mill
6. Ignore feedback
7. Emphasize techniques (rather than results)
8. Implement overnight
9. Fail to reward
10. Have objectives but no plans
11. Stick with original program
12. Be impatient
13. Quantify everything
14. Stress objectives, not the system
15. Dramatize short-term objectives
16. Omit periodic reviews
17. Omit refresher training
18. Don't blend objectives
19. Be gutless
20. Refuse to delegate

If you do it right, though, there are many benefits to the establishment of an MBO program. Some of these benefits include the following:

(a) Increased motivation of employees *and* managers

(b) More time for managers to manage due to the group effort toward meeting goals

(c) Clear-cut goals making it easier for managers and employees to devote their time to activities that have the greatest pay-off for the company

(d) Improved coordination and teamwork among all personnel

(e) More equitable salary distribution since compensation is based on results

(f) Improved communication since the entire company is working toward mutual goals

(g) Easier performance evaluation since performance is judged by specific accomplishments, not subjective or generalized opinions

Perhaps the most difficult and challenging — and the most important — aspect of the MBO system is goal setting. When establishing goals in an MBO program, you should keep the following in mind:

(a) Goals should support the overall objectives

(b) Goals should relate both to the objectives at higher levels and the goals at lower levels

(c) Results, not activities, should be defined

(d) Focus on the job, not the person in the job

(e) Goals should be challenging

(f) There should be an emphasis on realism

(g) Goals should recognize constraints

(h) Goals should function as tools to measure and control performance

(i) The most important goals should be given the most weight

(j) Use language that everyone will understand

(k) Provide flexibility for change

Devote plenty of time to implementation, proceed in a gradual manner, and thoroughly digest each bite before taking another one. That's the way to make MBO work!

g. QUALITY OF WORK LIFE — THE COMPANY MEETING THE EMPLOYEES' NEEDS

The term "Quality of Work Life" or QWL has been around for a long time but, like the other programs we've looked at, really did not gain momentum until the 1970s.

In 1972, the first international QWL Conference attracted only 50 people. In 1981 there were more than 1500 delegates, including 200 unionists and 750 practicing managers.

1. What is a Quality of Work Life program?

QWL is a term that refers to how well a job or the job environment matches the needs of its workers. The purpose of a quality of work life program is to produce more humanized jobs — jobs that increase worker satisfaction. When a QWL program is established, jobs are redesigned, organizational relationships are changed, and the work environment is altered to make work a better place for everyone.

QWL programs are based on the idea that workers need to be allowed to meet their higher order needs: the needs of esteem, recognition, self-improvement, and growth, as well as the more basic needs. The job and work environment is structured to meet as many of the workers' needs as possible. The work is meaningful for the employees. The job doesn't put the workers under unnecessary stress. Instead, the job contributes to the workers' ability to grow in other life roles.

2. How does a QWL program work?

To humanize the *work* that employees do, a company must —

(a) increase the variety of work done by each employee,

(b) allow employees to complete whole tasks rather than parts of tasks,

(c) make the tasks that employees are required to do meaningful,

(d) increase the autonomy of employees so that they are working self-sufficiently, and

(e) provide frequent feedback.

To humanize the *work environment*, a company must —

(a) share power within the organization rather than setting up a rigid structure, and

(b) allow flexible work schedules and provide options like flextime, compressed workweeks, and job sharing.

3. Making a QWL program work

Case histories of QWL organizations show they can improve product quality and productivity, reduce absenteeism and turnover, and increase job satisfaction.

QWL is not, however, a "quick-fix." There are several reasons that such a program may not work:

(a) Lack of management commitment

(b) Employee apathy

(c) Failure to understand the philosophy the program is based on

Almost everyone in the organization must understand, believe in, and commit to QWL for it to work.

When establishing a QWL program you should make sure that —

(a) management understands what QWL is all about and is willing to make a large, long-range commitment,

(b) you enlist the help of a consultant in organizational development,

(c) you train and retrain *everybody* in the company, and

(d) you begin your QWL efforts on a limited scale that focuses on the solution of specific problems.

h. CONCLUSION

There are countless examples of companies dedicated to encouraging participation and involvement among their employees. These are all companies that are aware of the needs of the employee in the nineties and take steps to fulfill those needs. These companies have benefited by this commitment to their human resource and have motivated this vital resource with a very powerful, nonmonetary incentive — involvement. You can too.

PART III
SPECIAL MOTIVATION
PROGRAMS/STRATEGIES

As we've already seen, the worker of the nineties is very different from the worker of the sixties, seventies, and even eighties. These differences mean we need new and creative approaches to motivation; we must focus on meeting the different needs of changing lifestyles.

Many innovative techniques have developed for these workers in recent years because more and more companies are concerned today with motivating their employees. And rightly so. Managers realize that the key to a productive workforce is productive employees. Further, they now understand that employees won't be productive if they're not motivated.

At Warner-Lambert Canada, for example, employees are offered a number of programs ranging from scholarship programs for their children and assistance in retirement planning to counseling on everything from substance abuse to family conflict and personal finances. After retirement, former employees continue to be welcomed at company-sponsored outings and community projects. And while the company freely admits that it is not the highest-paying pharmaceutical company in the country, its turnover rate is low for the industry.

Much of the process of motivating employees involves the day-to-day business of setting goals, providing feedback, involving employees in decisions, and recognizing their efforts. These techniques are becoming the norm.

Beyond those "standards," however, lies a wealth of strategies that some of the more successful companies in North America are using. You can easily incorporate some of these strategies into your management system. We'll take a look at some of these less traditional methods in this section.

9
JOB ENRICHMENT

Not everyone likes everything about their jobs. In fact, some people don't like *anything* about the job they do. You probably know some of these people. You probably have some of them working in your organization, perhaps even working for you.

What do you do with people who don't seem to like what they do? Who don't perform to capacity? Who come in late, call in sick, are slow in production?

If you're truly interested in providing a motivating environment for all of your employees your answer won't be "fire them" because terminations are dis-motivating, not only for the person being terminated but also for the workers who keep their jobs, and in many cases, it isn't the employee that's the problem anyway — it's the job itself.

Herzberg said, "The proper attitude for a man in a Mickey Mouse job is a Mickey Mouse attitude." Many theorists agree with him, at least in principle.

Michael Maccoby, a prominent behavioral scientist, says:

> In general, workers want to avoid jobs that are monotonous, repetitive, over-controlled, and isolated from interaction with others. In contrast, they seek jobs that require activeness — planning and judgment — autonomy on the job, variety and that are demanding enough to stimulate learning. Beyond these

psychological factors, workers are also concerned with the dignity associated with the job and with opportunities for career development. They are also increasingly concerned that the work be "meaningful," that it involve clearly useful tasks and require sufficient skills to be worthy of respect.

Taken together, these requirements move in the direction of humanizing work. In contrast, dehumanized work is a job which makes the worker into a machine part, totally controlled, fully predictable and easily replaceable.

A good job will provide the following:

(a) Natural units of work. Employees will be able to see a beginning and an end to their tasks.

(b) Meaningful goals. Clear and moderately difficult goals give employees something to shoot for. Participation in goal setting encourages commitment instead of compliance. Goals should be set high enough to be challenging. Goals shouldn't be so high, however, that they are impossible to reach.

(c) Direct feedback. A goal is meaningful only if employees can get quick, direct information on how they're doing. It's best if this feedback can come from the work itself.

(d) Client relationship. Employees should have direct contact with the users of their products or services. These users may be inside or outside the company.

(e) Autonomy (decision-making discretion). Jobs should be designed so jobholders are involved in setting their schedules, choosing work methods, troubleshooting, checking on quality, training other workers, and problem-solving.

Turning "a job" into "a good job" involves the process of job enrichment. Job enrichment is the enlargement of a job's responsibility, scope, and challenge. An enriched job will meet an employee's needs for achievement, recognition, satisfaction, responsibility, growth, and advancement. The most effective job enrichment approaches are either programs that change the employee's day-to-day job, or programs that increase employee participation in decisions affecting their work.

Many employees respond to job enrichment because it makes their job more interesting, challenging, and satisfying. Enrichment techniques change the content of the job. This is done by increasing employee autonomy, decision-making responsibility, skills used, the completeness of the tasks performed, and the amount of direct feedback.

Keep in mind, however, that job enrichment is not for everyone. At Motorola employees were given the chance of remaining on the traditional assembly line or assembling the whole product on a bench by themselves. Half of the 60 workers chose to stay on the assembly line.

Employees vary in their response to job enrichment. You should let employees decide whether they want their higher-order needs to be satisfied, and in what ways. Forcing someone into an enriched job can cause increased absenteeism, poorer work quality, and reduced output.

Walton lists six crucial factors for successful job enrichment:

1. Internal consistency

2. Continued support from upper management

3. Continued service of consultants or leaders working with the project

4. Absence of stress and crisis

5. Good relations between the work unit and other parts of the organization

6. Diffusion to other parts of the organization

Job enrichment can take several forms. We'll discuss job redesign (including both job enlargement and job restructuring), team efforts, and participation, plus two relatively new approaches to job enrichment: job sharing and flextime scheduling.

a. JOB REDESIGN

Many jobs are poorly designed. They do not help productivity or encourage employee enthusiasm. The problem lies in job design. The traditional approach to job design has been based on five general rules:

1. Skills should be specialized

2. Skill requirements should be minimized

3. Training time should be minimized

4. The number and variety of tasks in a job should be limited

5. The job should be as repetitive as possible

This approach to job design creates a position that is, in effect, too easy. Dividing work into parts that are too small leads to over-specialization which in turn can cause boredom, fatigue, apathy, absenteeism, grievances, reduced productivity, work stoppages, and high turnover. Specialization uses only a portion of worker abilities. The result — bored, unenthusiastic workers who eventually "give up."

Jobs need to be designed so that workers —

(a) are given responsibilities and challenges that match their skills, abilities, and expectations,

(b) can experience a wholeness to their work,

(c) can more easily identify their contributions to the organization's objectives,

(d) can participate in decisions that affect their jobs, and

(e) control larger portions of their own work.

Job redesign involves redefining a job. Employees are given greater responsibility, allowed more control, and provided with frequent feedback. There are two broad aspects to job redesign: job enlargement and job restructuring.

1. Job enlargement

Job enlargement increases the number of tasks assigned to an employee. The employee's autonomy, decision-making authority, or skill level is not increased.

Job enlargement broadens the job rather than deepening the employee's responsibility. By increasing the variety of tasks, an employee is called upon to use a greater variety of knowledge and skill and is allowed more freedom and responsibility. This is often called horizontal job enrichment. For example, instead of ten workers each doing one step in a process, each worker might perform all steps and inspect the completed job.

Companies considering job enlargement programs are usually trying to reduce boredom while improving the quality of the products produced. Job enlargement makes work more interesting and challenging and aids in cost reduction.

Choosing a motivated employee is a key factor in the success of job enlargement.

2. Job restructuring

Job restructuring is an attempt to increase the depth of a job by requiring higher knowledge and skill. This is sometimes called vertical job enrichment. It gives employees added opportunity for planning and controlling their work. The idea is that employees can manage themselves quite well if allowed to. Jobs are expanded to allow workers to participate in managerial functions like planning and controlling. Employees use their own judgment and discretion to make decisions about their work. They participate with their supervisors in problem solving and goal setting. They offer ideas, suggestions, and opinions. The employee is given greater autonomy and increased responsibility for planning, directing, and controlling the work done.

b. TEAM EFFORTS

Team efforts are programs designed to bring employees together to work as a single group. There are different types of teams that can be formed:

Operating teams — groups of employees who perform their day-to-day tasks as a team

Problem-oriented teams and task forces — groups of employees who come together on a temporary or permanent basis to discuss and recommend solutions to specific problems

Management teams — groups of supervisory and management personnel who work together regularly to deal with operational problems, daily decisions, or specific objectives

These type of work teams allow employees who might not otherwise have the opportunity to contribute their thoughts and ideas to do so. Employees who previously only "did their jobs" can now play an integral role in shaping procedures and policies and improving operations by becoming involved as part of a group that is given the authority to make decisions.

c. INCREASED PARTICIPATION

Participation usually involves labor-management committees or participative decision making. Labor-management committees let employee unions or associations deal constructively with management on such issues as productivity, working conditions, and safety. These committees often include rank and file employees.

Participative decision making involves techniques that give line employees a chance to influence managerial decisions. These techniques range from the establishment of employee advisory roles to employee veto power on managerial decisions.

d. JOB ROTATION

Job rotation provides employees with experiences in different jobs on a regular basis. Rotation can be within or between departments. Employees switch from one job to another. Job rotation provides variety and helps prevent boredom. The content of the job remains unchanged.

Job rotation lets employees share unexciting or repetitive tasks. It's important to note, however, that job rotation won't work if employees are simply rotated from one repetitive job to another.

e. JOB SHARING

Job sharing allows two or three employees to fill a job. They share the job's salary and benefits. Job holders are able to use their experience and education on less than a fulltime basis.

An American Management Society (AMS) study indicated that 80% of U.S. companies with job-sharing plans pay workers the same hourly rate as full-time workers.

In a job-sharing arrangement, two or more people may share a single fulltime job. For example, two people may share a 40-hour-per-week job. One person might work from 8 a.m. to noon, the other person from 1 p.m. to 5 p.m. each day. Or perhaps each person might work 2½ days.

Research shows that not only are turnover and absenteeism lower in job-shared jobs, but productivity is higher. In fact, productivity can sometimes be up to 25% higher.

When developing a job-sharing program, keep the following guidelines in mind:

(a) Choose participants whose skills are complementary.

(b) Be sure that all workers are very well organized.

(c) Don't overlook the possibility of job sharing between supervisors and assistants.

(d) Make it clear to each employee involved that he or she is responsible for the *whole* job, not just his or her percentage.

f. FLEXTIME

Flextime (also known as flexitime and flexible scheduling) allows employees to work schedules that consist of two parts. The first part is a base period, often called "core time," when everyone must be at work. The second part is a flexible period, usually at the beginning or ending of each work shift. Employees can choose their arrival and departure times.

Flexibility lets night owls and early birds work the hours they're most sharp. The typical 9 to 5 schedule works for almost nobody. Flextime schedules can suit each individual employee.

The use of flextime programs is growing. In 1977, only 15% of companies surveyed had flextime programs. But by late 1985, an AMS survey of 280 U.S. companies showed that 28% were using flextime. Another 5% were considering a flextime program.

Some of the most prestigious corporations have successful programs:

- At Hewlett-Packard you can start work at 6:00 a.m., 7:00 a.m., or 8:00 a.m.

- Control Data notes that tardiness and absenteeism decreased since the advent of flextime.

- Fox Jones & Associates, a company of consultants in Toronto, has a unique plan. Employee benefits include as much vacation as the employees want. The founder, Jeremy Fox, feels the policy actually increases productivity, encouraging employees to organize their time more efficiently, project by project rather than day by day.

- Metropolitan Life of New York, a flextime employer since 1974, reports increased productivity when workers schedule their own hours.

- Conoco in Houston switched to flextime in 1976. People there like arriving as early as 6:45 a.m. because they can get a lot done before the telephones start ringing.

- Meredith, the Des Moines-based publisher of magazines such as *Better Homes and Gardens* and *Metropolitan Home*, uses flextime in the office and the compressed workweek in the pressrooms.

There are, of course, both positive and negative aspects to a flextime work schedule. Participants in the AMS survey were asked about the advantages and disadvantages of flextime.

Advantages:

- Improves employee attitude and morale

- Accommodates working parents

- Workers can avoid rush-hour traffic

- Increases production

- Decreases tardiness

- Accommodates those who wish to arrive at work before interruptions begin

- Helps employees schedule medical, dental, and other appointments

- Decreases absenteeism

- Accommodates leisure-time activities of employees
- Decreases turnover

Disadvantages:

- Lack of supervision during all hours of work
- Having key people unavailable at times
- Occasional understaffing
- Meetings are sometimes difficult to schedule
- Employee abuse of flextime program
- Keeping track of hours worked
- Planning work schedules is difficult
- It can be hard to coordinate projects

g. INTRODUCING A JOB ENRICHMENT PROGRAM

Job enrichment is an important way to mesh today's business needs with the needs of employees. Businesses need able and loyal workers. Workers need to meet their higher order needs. Job enrichment works for both of them.

J. Richard Hackman of Yale, job redesign authority, and his associates say, "When these…conditions are present, a person tends to feel very good about himself when he performs well. And those good feelings will prompt him to try to continue to do well — so he can continue to earn the positive feelings in the future. That is what is meant by 'internal motivation' — being turned on to one's work because of the positive internal feelings that are generated by doing well, rather than being dependent on external factors…"

They have identified five core characteristics of jobs that will motivate people to be high performers: skill variety, task identity (that is, the degree to which the job involves the

completion of a whole and identifiable task), task signifi-
cance, autonomy, and feedback. They have also identified
five parallel strategies for changing the job to make it more
meaningful. These strategies and the questions to ask when
trying to implement them are outlined below.

1. **Form natural work units to promote the employee's
   sense of "ownership"**

Ask yourself:

(a) Does the job correspond to a natural unit of work, one
    in which the employee can develop a sense of contin-
    uing responsibility?

(b) Is there any basis for identifying the job with the
    person or department for whom it is performed?

(c) Is work assigned randomly or naturally — in ways
    that promote task identity?

2. **Combine separate tasks wherever possible**

Ask yourself:

(a) Can separate tasks be combined into larger work
    units?

(b) Can tasks like setup, inspection, verification, or
    checking be added to existing work units?

(c) Can responsibility for a new, larger task be assigned
    to a small team of workers?

3. **Establish client relationships to expand the three
   core dimensions of feedback, skill variety,
   and autonomy**

Ask yourself:

(a) Do we know who the client for the worker's services
    is?

(b) Can we establish direct contact between the worker
    and the client?

140

(c) Can we set up criteria so the client can judge the quality of the product or service?

(d) Can we give the client a way of communicating evaluations directly to employees?

4. Give rank-and-file employees management-type responsibilities

Ask yourself:

(a) Can we give workers more responsibility for setting schedules, deciding on work methods, and helping to train less experienced employees?

(b) Can we give workers more control over their time — when to stop and start work, take breaks, etc.?

(c) Can we encourage workers to come up with problem solutions on their own rather than relying on their bosses for the answers?

(d) Can we provide the workers with more information about the financial aspects of their jobs?

5. Open feedback channels so workers can learn about performance while doing the job

Ask yourself:

(a) Can we place quality control close to the workers so they get frequent feedback on performance?

(b) Can we provide workers directly with standard summaries of performance records?

(c) Can workers receive individual performance information via computer instead of secondhand?

(d) Can workers correct their own mistakes?

h. A MODEL

Robert N. Ford gives a "Model for Maximum Job Motivation" in *Why Jobs Die and What to Do About It* (AMACOM, 1979). This model is useful in job redesign.

(a) Let employees know what the organization's objectives are.

(b) Let them know how their segment is performing with respect to purpose and objectives.

(c) Start them on some part of the segment — a "slice of the business."

(d) Let them have maximum control over what they do.

(e) Let them do as much of the job of fulfilling the purpose of the business segment as they can.

(f) If this is helpful, organize self-contained work units, or mini-groups of mutually supporting workers.

(g) Give employees lots of feedback as to how they are doing.

(h) Give access to staff support for information and expertise.

(i) Give access to the boss for knowledge and support.

i. MONITORING THE PROGRAM

Supervisors always need to watch for such trouble signs as high turnover, restricted output, poor quality, and excessive absenteeism. When working toward job enrichment, keep in mind the following points:

(a) Tasks that challenge without overwhelming or underestimating the person will tend to be more motivating.

(b) The chances for employees to become involved in their work are greater if control of the work (power to act, responsibility, and authority) is moved downward to the employees rather than upward to the boss.

(c) Feedback from an aspect of the work itself is a far better reinforcer of good performance than is feedback through a superior.

(d) Employees are more likely to accept added responsibility if appropriate feedback and control are included.

(e) A total job redesign effort that starts at the bottom of an organization is easier and more natural to effect than a job enrichment effort that starts at the top.

(f) The job will motivate most which best meets the current needs of an employee.

(g) Let all employees participate, but in well-planned stages.

(h) Don't sell the idea of big improvements in a short time; sell the idea of a long, slow pull upward.

(i) Concentrate on existing jobs first.

(j) Work on jobs in the mainstream of the organization rather than on the "safe" jobs.

(h) Begin with work groups where the team of managers is likely to remain relatively intact for the period of the project.

(i) Drop no current job procedures until a substitute is ready.

(j) Give employees new responsibilities, even if there is a doubt about their readiness.

(k) Encourage the organization to build a ladder of good jobs, a career path, with the potential for motivating people for years.

10
FLEXIBLE BENEFITS

Janelle is 18, not very concerned about her retirement, but wishing she had more than one week of vacation to use. What with "spring break" and hot summer afternoons, a week just doesn't seem like much time.

Doug is 58 and concerned about the future needs of himself and his wife as they approach retirement age. He wishes his company would offer some form of retirement/savings plan that would allow him to contribute a portion of his income on a tax-deferred basis and perhaps offer a reciprocal contribution from the company as well.

Sandy is 35 and a single mother of two. Not only is daycare expensive and eating up her limited disposable income, but she finds it difficult to be away from her children all day. She thinks it would be great if her company offered daycare benefits of some sort.

Bob is 42 and married with four children, and his wife is pregnant. His most fervent wish? That his company would offer a more generous health-care program. His doctor and dentist expenses are crippling him and he'd gladly trade in a couple of weeks of vacation for more extensive health coverage.

Janelle, Doug, Sandy, and Bob are all good examples of the employee of the nineties. They demonstrate that packaged benefit programs simply don't meet the needs of today's very different individuals.

We've already seen that employees are uniquely motivated. They're also unique in their need for various "traditional" employee benefits.

Vacation, sick pay, and health insurance are almost considered "standard" as far as benefits go. Most companies have established policies in place for how these benefits are distributed and it usually works something like this: one week of paid vacation after one full year of employment, eligible for health plan immediately — choice between individual plan (completely paid by company) or family plan (company pays 50%).

This is all well and good as far as it goes, but it's as futile to apply the same benefit strategies to all employees as it is to apply the same motivational strategies.

American businesses have historically designed their benefit programs for the "traditional" family where Dad goes to work every day and Mom stays home to care for the children. But, as we all know, things are changing. Employers are finding that a decreasing number of their employees fit the "typical" mold of the forties, fifties, and sixties.

Enter the "cafeteria" or flexible benefits plan — a plan that not only serves the individual needs of employees but, in many cases, saves money for the employer as well.

a. HOW DOES A FLEXIBLE BENEFIT PLAN WORK?

The first flexible benefit programs were implemented in 1974 by the Educational Testing Service and a division of TRW, an automotive products remanufacturing company in Cleveland, Ohio. American Can, a packaging company, then developed a program which was tested in 1978 and started in 1979. Since then, a number of companies have established flexible benefit plans. These companies include Morgan Stanley, Northern States Power, Fluor, Loews, Marriott, Mellon Bank, Comerica, First Bank System, Chemical Bank, LTV,

145

Pepsico, Quaker Oats, and many others. By early 1988 their number had reached 466.

"Cafeteria" plans accommodate the needs of today's work force by allowing individual choice from among several benefit options. Employees receive credits or "flexible compensation dollars" to spend on the benefits *they* want. They aren't forced to accept fixed benefits as part of a standard employment package.

These credits are called "flexible compensation dollars" because they are —

(a) *flexible* — employees can spend their credits on the benefits they most need and want,

(b) *compensation* — the credits are part of an employee's wage or salary package, the portion traditionally known simply as benefits and not included in gross pay, and

(c) *dollars* — employees spend their credits in much the same way they would spend money at a cafeteria for lunch — a little vacation time, a lot of health insurance, skip the legal services, etc.

When a "cafeteria" program is established, a company will give a specific level of benefit credits to employees. This amount is often based on length of service, job classification, salary, or other factors. Employees then spend credits to establish their own customized benefit plan. If they spend less than their total credits, they may take cash. The cash is then taxable. If they want more benefits, they may convert some of their pre-tax salary into benefits.

Almost any tax-free benefit, except educational assistance, may be included in these programs. These tax-free benefits usually include —

- Medical expense reimbursement

- Accident, health, and hospitalization

- Disability insurance

- Group term life insurance

- Group legal services

- Dependent care assistance

Taxable benefits (except cash) may also be included. As we will see, though, there is no practical benefit to either employee or employer to do so.

The move toward "cafeteria" plans meets both employer and employee needs. For the employee, a cafeteria plan offers the opportunity for increased control over benefits and the ability to custom-fit these benefits to individual needs. It also offers the opportunity to save money on previously uncovered expenses with tax breaks that only a company program can make possible.

b. SAMPLES OF FLEXIBLE BENEFITS

1. Childcare

Dan is widowed and supporting two pre-school children. In the past he has paid for childcare with money he receives each week from his check — his "take-home" pay or taxable income. This money has already been reduced by deductions for state and federal income tax and Social Security tax. Through the "cafeteria" program recently implemented at the company Dan works for, he is able to choose childcare from the benefits offered. The flexible compensation dollars he spends for childcare are *not* included in his gross income. Therefore, this amount is not taxed. The tax saving Dan realizes can mean a significant increase in his take-home pay.

As you can see, the major benefit that "cafeteria" programs provide for employees is the opportunity to pay for items such as daycare (or legal expenses or non-covered health expenditures) with pre-tax dollars — that is, dollars that are not included in taxable salary. Since these benefits are not considered taxable income, the workers are not pushed into a higher tax bracket.

If they wish, employees may convert their flexible compensation dollars to cash which will be taxed. Employers, of course, hope that their employees don't do this. It is the conversion of taxable income to tax-free benefits that saves money for both employer and employee.

2. Retirement savings

Jeff and Jane both work fulltime at XYZ Corporation. They have no dependents and do not own their home. Their combined income puts them in a very high tax bracket. They would like to lower their tax bracket and save for their retirement at the same time. By converting some of their taxable income into non-taxed "flexible compensation dollars" which they spend on the employee retirement program they are able to do just that. They have saved. XYZ Corporation has also saved.

c. OPTING OUT OF UNWANTED BENEFITS

"Cafeteria" plans save employers money not only in income tax and social security payments, but also by reducing the amount of benefits which are paid for in traditional plans but not used by employees. This is money that is usually "thrown away" by the employer.

For example, Sara is 21 years old. She's a single college student and has worked at Widget Company for a little over a year. Her primary interest in the "cafeteria" plan is to have more vacation time each year. Because she is usually in good health and makes infrequent visits to the doctor, she chooses a low health care plan. She also chooses the minimal life insurance coverage and disability insurance.

Joe, 43, has been with ABC Manufacturing for 10 years. His wife, Elaine, does not have a job but stays home to care for their three children. Because the medical expenses of raising a family have become hard to bear, he wants the best medical coverage he can get. He'd also like to save money for retirement.

d. ESTABLISHING A FLEXIBLE BENEFITS PLAN

For employers thinking of establishing a flexible benefits plan, the most important considerations are the following:

(a) Develop employee understanding so the plan is used. This will result in savings for both employee and employer. Employers *don't* want their employees to choose cash (which is taxable) instead of choosing from the other available options.

(b) Provide a core of benefits so employees receive adequate coverage.

(c) Determine whether the savings will outweigh the costs.

(d) Monitor changes in tax laws.

Determining what benefits to include may at first seem to be a major task. For many companies, however, it has involved no more than a brief survey to determine which benefits employees are most likely to take advantage of. The results of such a survey allow management to determine the best way to set up their "cafeteria" program. You could use Worksheet #3 to determine the needs and desires of your own employees.

Obviously, before starting a flexible benefits plan, a company must determine whether expected savings will offset the costs. Most companies feel that these programs are cost effective.

Another important factor is employee understanding. The options available and tax implications involved can be confusing. If employees do not understand the plan, they will not make use of it. Then, neither the employee nor the employer will save anything in the process.

Is it worth it? It seems to be.

The Wyatt Company, the largest independent employee benefit consulting firm in the U.S., has established "cafeteria" programs for several major companies. They have found that management is able to achieve business objectives that include —

(a) reducing short-term costs (i.e., state, federal, and social security taxes),

(b) controlling long-term costs (such as increasing expenditures for employee benefits),

(c) getting and keeping good employees,

(d) reducing the appeal of unionization to the workforce, and

(e) providing a framework to unify benefit plans and establish corporate identity.

Companies throughout the United States and Canada are finding that "cafeteria" programs are a godsend, in terms of both tax savings and employee satisfaction. They are just one more element in the development of a motivated workforce.

WORKSHEET #4
EMPLOYEE BENEFITS SURVEY

From the list of employee benefits below, please indicate those benefits that *you believe* are provided by your employer at this time.

BENEFIT OFFERED	Definitely	Maybe	No
Overtime pay for holidays	☐	☐	☐
Sick pay	☐	☐	☐
Personal holidays	☐	☐	☐
Retirement benefits (pension plan)	☐	☐	☐
Hospitalization insurance	☐	☐	☐
Dental insurance	☐	☐	☐
Optical	☐	☐	☐
Life insurance	☐	☐	☐
Funeral leave pay	☐	☐	☐
Tuition reimbursement	☐	☐	☐
Leave of absence	☐	☐	☐
Paid lunch breaks	☐	☐	☐
Paid coffee breaks	☐	☐	☐
Profit-sharing payments	☐	☐	☐
Payment of counseling fees	☐	☐	☐
Social events	☐	☐	☐
Flower fund	☐	☐	☐
Paid seminar observation	☐	☐	☐

BENEFIT OFFERED	Definitely	Maybe	No
Paid educational Workshops/seminars	☐	☐	☐
Disability insurance	☐	☐	☐
Jury duty leave pay	☐	☐	☐

Other (e.g., in the U.S., vacation pay, paid holidays, pharmacy service, social security, unused vacation paid at termination of employment, military reserve duty pay, maternity leave benefits)

_____

_____

_____

The same benefits are listed below. Please indicate, based on the scale provided, *how important* each benefit is to you regardless of whether it is offered by your employer.

1 = not important
2 = somewhat important
3 = important
4 = very important
5 = extremely important

Overtime pay for holidays _____

Sick pay _____

Personal holidays _____

Retirement benefits (pension plan) _____

Hospitalization insurance _____

Dental insurance _____

Optical   _____

Life insurance   _____

Funeral leave pay   _____

Tuition reimbursement   _____

1 = not important
2 = somewhat important
3 = important
4 = very important
5 = extremely important

Leave of absence   _____

Paid lunch breaks   _____

Paid coffee breaks   _____

Profit-sharing payments   _____

Payment of counseling fees   _____

Social events   _____

Flower fund   _____

Paid seminar observation   _____

Paid educational workshops/seminars   _____

Disability insurance   _____

Jury duty leave pay   _____

Other (e.g., in the U.S., vacation pay, paid holidays, pharmacy service, social security, unused vacation paid at
termination of employment, military reserve duty pay,
maternity leave benefits)

List those identified in the first list that are not listed above and rate their level of importance:

Other (specify)

_____

_____

_____

Based on the benefits that you feel are provided by your employer, please estimate:

    1. The dollar cost per hour per employee these benefits cost your employer — $_____ per hour

    2. The dollar cost per year per employee these benefits cost your employer — $_____ per year

Using the scale below please indicate your answers to the following questions:

1 = not important
2 = somewhat important
3 = important
4 = very important
5 = extremely important

1. How important were the benefits offered by your employer to you when you applied for employment? _____

2. How important are the benefits offered by your employer to you in your decision to stay employed at the company? _____

3. How important do you feel the benefits offered by your employer are in encouraging each employee to do a good job? _____

4. How important do you feel the benefits offered are in satisfying your economic needs in ways which your straight wages cannot? _____

The following questions are designed to gather some demographic information which allows us to summarize your answers and determine the general feelings of groups.

1. Your sex is: ❏ female   ❏ male

2. Your age is: _____

3. Your education level is:

    ❏ less than high school

    ❏ high school graduate

    ❏ some college or technical school

    ❏ vocational school or junior college graduate

    ❏ college graduate

    ❏ college graduate plus

4. Your length of employment with your current employer is:_____

5. Marital status: ❏ married   ❏ single
                   ❏ widowed or divorced

6. Age(s) of children living at home: _____

_____

7. If you are married, does your spouse have a fringe benefit package similar to yours? ❑ yes ❑ no

8. Your income excluding fringe benefits:

      ❑ under $10,000

      ❑ 10,001 - 15,000

      ❑ 15,001 - 20,000

      ❑ 20,001 - 25,000

      ❑ 25,001 - 30,000

      ❑ 30,001 - 35,000

      ❑ 35,001 - 40,000

      ❑ over 40,000

9. Your total family income (sum of yours and spouse). If no spouse contributing to family income skip this question.

      ❑ under $20,000

      ❑ 20,001 - 25,000

      ❑ 25,001 - 30,000

      ❑ 30,001 - 35,000

      ❑ 35,001 - 40,000

      ❑ 40,001 - 45,000

      ❑ 45,001 - 50,000

      ❑ 50,001 - 55,000

      ❑ 55,001 - 60,000

❏ 60,001 - 65,000

❏ 65,001 - 70,000

❏ 70,001 - 75,000

❏ 75,001 - 80,000

❏ over 80,000

10. Number of hours you work per week for this organization:

_____

11. Do you currently work for another company(s)?
❏ yes ❏ no   If yes, how many other companies?

_____

How many hours in total do you work for these other companies (per week)? _____

12. Answer this question only if you are employed part time by this organization. Do you currently wish to work full time for this organization at the same hourly wage rate? ❏ very much ❏ yes ❏ somewhat ❏ no ❏ definitely not

11
EMPLOYEE ASSISTANCE PROGRAMS

For several months, almost everyone on the staff of XYZ Corporation has been aware that Joe is having personal problems. Not only has his personal appearance declined, but he is calling in sick more and more often, especially on Mondays after payday, doing very little work on the days he does show up, and rapidly becoming snappy and irritable. After several complaints from coworkers (and a few from disgruntled customers), Joe's supervisor, Sharon, is beginning to suspect that Joe has a drinking problem.

A recent federally supported six-year study of 20,000 people in the United States found that 18.7% of the adults suffered from at least one mental health disorder during an average six-month period. For managers, this figure is frightening, because it means that the chances of being responsible for an employee who has a drug, alcohol, or psychological problem are very good.

Working with "troubled" employees can be one of the most challenging and frustrating aspects of managerial jobs. Many hospitals and corporations are now establishing formal programs to help managers and their employees. Employee Assistance Programs or EAPs are systems which provide professional services to employees whose job performance is or may become adversely affected by any number of factors including substance abuse, emotional problems, family difficulties, legal issues, physical health disorders, and/or similar personal problems. These problems not only threaten the employee's effectiveness on the job but also tend to trigger a wide range of health problems (physical and emotional) as well as disrupting the performance of other employees.

EAPs can either be on-site, staffed by trained counselors, or as is most often the case, off-site and accessible to a number of companies and their employees. EAPs provide assistance by using resources already available in the community: attorneys, marriage counselors, addiction counselors, financial counselors, psychologists, and so on.

Employees may be referred to the EAP by their supervisor or manager or may use "self-referral." Managers who use EAPs to help their employees deal with problems are not "prying." Their concern is bringing the employee's job performance back up to standard. All interaction of an employee with an EAP is confidential.

EAPs aren't anything new. In 1917, Macy's Department Store established a program to help employees deal with their personal problems. However, EAPs are becoming increasingly popular. Thousands of companies in the U.S. and Canada are using these programs to provide assistance to millions of employees.

While earlier programs had a focus that was almost exclusively on alcoholism and drug-related problems, today's programs take a more holistic approach and focus on every aspect of the employee's life. The result has been that there is a greater recognition that everyone is susceptible to problems that can create on-the-job stress — that the presence of these problems is not a stigma. Consequently, today's programs are more successful because they are more often utilized.

a. HOW EAPs WORK

EAPs are based on the philosophy that employees are a valuable company resource that needs to be protected. Employee retention is one of the most notable results of an EAP.

Today's EAP is not just for employees. EAPs also serve the employee's family members, corporations, and communities. They are focused more on intervention and prevention rather than being crisis-oriented as they were when they first came into being.

EAPs give employees a confidential outlet for personal or job concerns. They are a way to help maintain existing staff by intervening before problems have a negative impact on a job situation and morale.

b. EAPs FROM THE MANAGER'S PERSPECTIVE

If an employee came to your office and confided in you that he or she was having marital problems and you responded, "unless it affects your performance on the job, your personal life doesn't interest me," what do you think would happen? Chances are, word would get around the company very quickly and you'd probably be looked upon by employees and coworkers as a poor manager.

But, let's suppose that instead you decided to spend some time working with that employee, helping him or her over the problems, counseling the employee during work hours, and being available after hours to empathize and "lend a shoulder." *Now* what do you think would happen? Chances are, word would get around the company very quickly and you'd probably be looked upon by employees and coworkers as a poor manager.

Hard to believe? Let's take a look at a typical situation.

You're the manager of a five-person department. One of your employees confides in you that he's having marital problems. "Pete" feels a separation is imminent but doesn't want anyone else to know about it. You promise to keep his situation confidential. He gets in the habit of stopping in to talk to you for 15 minutes or an hour almost every day.

Of course, the other four people in your department don't know why this employee is suddenly receiving preferential treatment. They begin to complain among themselves and others in the company that "Pete" is your "favorite." You spend a great deal of time with him and you've overlooked the fact that he's been late to work twice in the past week.

"Pete's" situation isn't getting any better with your counsel. His work is not improving. Your other employees are not being helped by this situation. Their work is not improving. For that matter, you are not being helped by this situation: your work is not improving either.

By spending extra time with an employee to work out "personal problems" you are —

(a) increasing the probability that you will be charged with "favoritism,"

(b) taking your valuable time away from the job your company is paying you to do,

(c) taking the troubled employee's valuable time away from the job your company is paying him or her to do, and

(d) taking all the rest of your employees' valuable time away from the job your company is paying them to do (because they're now busy gossiping and complaining about your non-work-related relationship with another employee).

The bottom line? You've damaged productivity and morale. And that's exactly what you set out to improve.

Supervisors and managers need to be cautious about becoming involved with their employees' personal problems. Professional distance must be maintained by supervisors. If you're trying to act as a counselor, you can't do it effectively, and by trying to do it you won't be able to hold effective performance evaluations as you're required to do.

Employee Assistance Programs allow companies to deal with personal problems *in*directly. Company time is not used to counsel troubled employees. Issues of "favoritism" are not raised. And, perhaps most importantly, the employee in question receives qualified professional help — help that can make a difference.

The supervisor's function in the EAP process is threefold:

1.   Provide information

2.   Encourage the use of EAPs

3.   Refer troubled employees

Even this limited involvement, however, can cause problems for managers.

c.   MANAGEMENT BARRIERS IN EMPLOYEE REFERRALS

There are a number of natural barriers that managers have in referring employees to EAPs.

1.   Reluctance to get involved

If a manager notices that an employee is becoming more and more withdrawn at work, she or he may hesitate to approach that employee. The manager may feel that, "It's a personal problem. It's not my place to get involved."

2.   Reluctance to interfere

Many times an employee's problem may not seem to directly affect performance. The manager doesn't want to "interfere" because "if it's not affecting his or her work, it's none of my business." The consequence may be, however, that the problem does ultimately affect performance.

3.   Reluctance to insult people

We've been taught since we were children that it's not polite to insult others. Approaching an employee who we suspect may have a personal problem may seem to us like the ulti-mate insult.

4. Willingness to bite the bullet

We're taught as managers to "bite the bullet." If an employee's work performance is declining due to personal problems, we may simply pitch in because "the work has to get done."

5. Desire to be nice

Many managers want to be perceived as "the nice guy." An employee who is consistently late to work because of childcare problems, for example, receives our empathy and "understanding." We don't consider the possibility that this employee may benefit from a visit to our EAP.

6. Lack of time

Face it. Most managers are strapped for time. Once they begin to become "involved" with the "personal" problems of em-ployees that time is at even a greater premium.

Let's take a further look at Joe's problem and Sharon's reaction to illustrate the five phases that a manager may go through before finally making the decision to refer an em-ployee to an EAP.

Uncertainty/denial: As we have seen, Sharon suspects that Joe is abusing alcohol. But when she approaches Joe, she receives a litany of excuses, "I've had car problems, family problems, marital problems..." You name it and Sharon's heard it. Sharon makes the decision that she "doesn't want to get involved" and gets Joe to promise that it won't happen again. She chooses to minimize the severity of the problem.

Anger, frustration, exasperation: Time passes and Joe continues to show up late. In addition, his performance has become sporadic and his temper even shorter. Sharon still doesn't "rock the boat" even though she's becoming more and more frustrated. She knows Joe has a lot of family problems — she wants to be "nice" and she doesn't want to insult Joe by implying that he can't handle his own personal life.

Guilt, self-doubt, and biting the bullet: At this stage, Sharon begins to question her own ability to deal with the situation. At the same time she feels guilty and inadequate. Joe's behavior is continuing to slide downward and now, in addition, the morale of the other workers in the department is declining and they're beginning to grumble about "special treatment." It's inventory time and everyone has to work harder to pull up Joe's slack.

Sharon begins to have more frequent confrontations with Joe and is spending too much of her time away from her duties as supervisor. But because she is so busy, Sharon feels she really can't spare the time right now to deal directly with Joe's problem.

Recognition: Sharon has finally realized that the efforts she's been making have not worked. She knows she needs to try a different course of action and, at this point, begins to consider the corporation's EAP as a possible solution. In order to be able to discuss the situation with Joe to everyone's best advantage, she finds out as much as she can about the EAPs available and talks to a EAP coordinator.

Referral: Sharon finally confronts Joe. After some argument, Joe admits, "I know I've been slipping, but I've been having some personal problems." Sharon responds by saying, "I understand how personal problems can affect your performance. While it's not my role to become involved in your personal life, I would like to refer you to the company EAP." Joe agrees. Sharon's continues to keep notes on Joe's performance and is pleased to find that his work subsequently improves.

d. YOUR ROLE AS A MANAGER

For managers, the decision to retain or fire an employee requires an ability to define job performance and measure progress toward recovery. Employee Assistance Programs have become an important means by which many companies are dealing with this problem.

In an article for the *Labor-Management Alcoholism Journal*, Professor Joan M. Gallagher of Boston College suggests several ways supervisors and managers can respond to the special needs of troubled employees:

(a) Accept the fact that a certain percentage of employees may not want to seek help through the company's program.

(b) Be readily available for private, confidential consultation.

(c) Promote attendance at educational conferences focusing on the specific interests and needs of the employee, such as a workshop on managerial stress.

(d) Encourage the employee to become involved in company programs which are attracting participation, such as the company's physical fitness program.

(e) Include spouses in educational and promotional efforts.

Managers need to understand what the EAP entails in some detail — how it affects you and your staff individually. Remember though — as a supervisor you are looking for increased *job* performance. You shouldn't need to know what the employee's specific problem is. When you confront a troubled employee, you don't want to talk about his or her personal life. You want to talk about job performance and how problems are exhibited on the job. While some employees may choose to "unload" on their managers, you must refrain from serving as counselor — you are not trained for this and intervening in this manner goes beyond your role as manager.

It's also important for managers to remember one of their major responsibilities is to document performance on the job and offers of help through EAP referral. You can't trust to memory the important facts that signaled a decline in performance. You should make a concerted effort to document any unusual occurrence — accidents, absences, missed meetings, missed deadlines, etc. Very often supervisors can't remember when a decline in performance started. Your documentation should include —

(a) name of employee,

(b) date of incident,

(c) explanation of the incident,

(d) names of others involved,

(e) action taken, and

(f) whether there was a discussion with the employee.

Be sure to document immediately after the incident. Don't rely on your memory to record the event later. Remember, you should be documenting only facts — observable, verifiable behaviors — not rumors, speculations, or guesses.

e. RECOGNIZING THE WARNING SIGNS

Employees don't develop problems overnight. In most cases, the supervisor should have been able to spot early warning signs well in advance of the need for action. When a problem is spotted at an early stage, it allows the opportunity for positive counseling and intervention before a major crisis develops.

What are some signs that a problem may be developing? There are several:

(a) There has been a decline in performance.

(b) The employee appears to be apathetic or withdrawn.

166

(c) The employee is a "whiner" — continually complaining about very trivial aspects of the job.

(d) You have found it difficult to establish a good working relationship with the employee.

(e) The employee is reluctant or refuses to discuss the problem.

(f) The employee has continuing interpersonal problems with others in the organization.

(g) The employee resents criticism.

(h) The employee's behavior is beginning to negatively affect others in the work group.

After these initial warning signals, the problem typically becomes more serious. At this stage you will be faced with more serious problems: absence without leave, disobedience, insubordination, or non-performance of job duties. When an employee problem has reached this stage, it's time to take action.

f. THE REFERRAL

A "troubled" employee will often go through a two-step intervention process:

1. The problem is referred to the appropriate person

The problem is identified and referred to the appropriate person. In Joe's case, action was taken due to complaints from fellow employees and customers. It is much better when the supervisor or manager is able to detect these problems at an earlier stage.

2. Warning interviews

Once the problem is identified, one or more warning interviews is held. The employee is given the choice of accepting a referral to the Employee Assistance Program or accepting the consequences of unacceptable job performance.

When you meet with an employee with the purpose of making a referral to your EAP, you should use job performance documentation as the basis for the referral. You shouldn't need to know the cause of the person's problem — that will not become known to you unless your employee signs a release for information to be released to you.

Choose the time and place for the meeting carefully. Allow plenty of time for the meeting so you will not be forced to rush. Make sure that you're able to meet in a private place. Avoid interruptions.

Make the employee feel important. Remember, this employee is a valuable company resource and the goal of the EAP is retention.

During the discussion, have thorough documentation present. Focus on the objective signs of performance that you've documented, not on the person. Stick to the facts. Allow the employee the opportunity to express his or her view but don't discuss or try to resolve the excuses. Remain objective. Don't lose your temper or become defensive.

Develop an action plan and set up checkpoints where you will measure performance improvements.

g. CONCLUSION

EAPs are not a cure-all and they don't always prove to be right for every organization. Difficulties in program implementation and on-going maintenance may result from managerial dissatisfaction over the number of self-referrals, inability or unwillingness on the part of supervisors and managers to refer employees, and dissatisfaction among employees concerning the way the program is run. Employees often express concerns over the issue of confidentiality.

Executive-level employees, especially, fear the repercussions of "word getting out" and the effects such knowledge might have on their standing in the company.

In general, however, employee assistance programs are proving to be a viable means of improving employee performance and retaining a company's valued resource — its personnel.

Employee Assistance Programs can benefit not only the troubled employee, but the employer as well. Both the cost effectiveness of these programs and the outstanding results demonstrated among troubled employees make EAPs an outlet which many organizations *should* look into and which more and more organizations *are* looking into.

12
WELLNESS/HEALTH PROGRAMS

At least two out of every five companies have health-awareness programs, according to a benefits survey by the Administrative Management Society. Of the 305 companies surveyed, close to half (42%) have formal health, physical fitness, or recreational programs. About 54% said they did not have such programs, while 4% are seriously considering them.

The price of success is high. It takes its toll upon today's workers in the form of ulcers, heart attacks, cancer, and other physical problems. Other symptoms include lethargy, irritability, and decreased productivity. Along with these nagging physical problems, employees often feel dissatisfaction with their job and may ultimately quit. This type of turnover is often blamed on "burnout."

a. JOB BURNOUT AND JOB STRESS

Sally is a nurse in a large hospital. Her hours are irregular. She deals daily with life and death situations. She must always be on her toes, ready to make quick decisions. She's been a nurse for the past 15 years. During the last two years, she has found it harder and harder to go to work. And, once at work, she's been making some minor mistakes — mistakes that may be affecting her future with the hospital.

Marsha is a copywriter. She says she really enjoys her work. She adds, however, "The deadlines can really drive you crazy. A lot of little things can really add up so you want to give up the whole works. Right now I love it — but I couldn't do this for the rest of my life."

Sally and Marsha are both suffering from job burnout. Although they're at different stages of the burnout process, their symptoms are quite similar.

Burnout is a debilitating psychological condition brought about by unrelieved work stress which results in —

(a) lowered energy reserves, exhaustion, and loss of enthusiasm,

(b) increased susceptibility to illness,

(c) dissatisfaction and pessimism, and

(d) increased absenteeism and inefficiency at work.

The causes of burnout are many. Often it is the result of a work situation where the person gets the feeling that he or she is beating his or her head against the wall day after day. It can result from boring work (boredom can cause burnout very quickly), lack of feedback, over-commitment, lack of recognition, unrealized self-expectations, or job pressure. There are four kinds of job pressure — too much work, pressure from superiors, deadlines, and low salaries.

Studies of burnout victims show they are hard working, dedicated, and idealistic. They are often a company's most valued workers — people who set high standards for themselves. For these employees, burnout can cause high blood pressure and family problems. From the employer's point of view, burnout can cause low productivity, increased absenteeism, and high turnover.

Job burnout is closely related to job stress. Every day, thousands of North Americans go home from work with nagging headaches, tense muscles, back problems, and other physical ailments. When they get home many of them must deal with more problems that try their patience and make them irritable.

What are they experiencing? Stress.

Stress lowers productivity. Statistics from the U.S. Clearinghouse for Mental Health show that the U.S. loses $17 billion annually in lost productivity due to stress. Other studies report even higher figures. Many employers have found that prevention can be far less costly than the lost productivity, errors, and accidents associated with stress.

b. HOW JOBS CONTRIBUTE TO STRESS

The first important consideration for employers is an awareness of the causes of stress. A number of things can cause a job situation to be stressful:

(a) *The job itself.* This includes too much or too little work, poor physical working conditions, and time pressure.

(b) *Role in the organization.* Employees may have problems with role conflict or confusion, responsibility for people, or lack of participation in decision making.

(c) *Career development.* This may involve under- or over-promotion, lack of job security, or unmet ambition.

(d) *Organizational structure and climate.* This factor involves lack of effective consultation, restrictions on behavior, and office politics.

(e) *Relationships within the organization.* If an employee has poor relationships with the boss, poor relationships with colleagues and subordinates, or difficulties in delegating responsibility, stress will be the result.

(f) *Extra-organizational sources.* Problems can arise over company vs. family demands, or company vs. an employee's own interests.

(g) *Managers* can trigger personality conflicts for employees. They may have an effect on an employee's ability to cope with change, motivation, and behavioral patterns. This depends on individual employees and individual personality traits.

172

Some jobs are more stressful than others. An evaluation of over 22,000 cases of stress-related health disorders in Tennessee showed high stress rates for 12 occupations. These occupations were: laborers, secretaries, inspectors, clinical lab technicians, office managers, managers/administrators, foremen, waitresses/waiters, machine operators, mine machine operators, and farm owners. Problems can be worse for women and minorities.

c. CREATING A LOW-STRESS ENVIRONMENT

As an employer, the first thing to try is providing a low-stress environment for your employees. There are many simple things you can do to establish such an environment. Here are just a few:

1. Ensure that job requirements are reasonably demanding

Both too high expectations and too low expectations can create stress. Employees need to be challenged, but not overwhelmed.

2. Provide opportunities for continued growth

If employees stop learning, they feel as though they're stagnating. That's how burnout develops. Consider methods of keeping your employees interested in their jobs, by providing them with opportunities to continue learning — cross-training, attendance at seminars, new responsibilities, etc.

3. Involve the employee in decision making

As we've already seen, employees like to be involved. By giving employees the opportunity to participate in decision making, they develop a feeling of control over their work and their futures. Lack of control is one of the largest contributing factors in the development of burnout.

4. Provide ample recognition and support

We've talked about this at length already, but it bears repeating. You can never offer too much praise as long as it's sincere.

5. Help employees to see the value in what they do

It's important that your employees see their jobs as contributing to the "big picture." They need to know that what they do matters and that what you do as a company is important and valuable. In short, they need to feel good about themselves and what they do. That's what motivation is all about.

Like many other employers, you'll probably find that results are favorable in terms of both the intangibles (like improved morale and company commitment) and the tangibles (like decreased health costs and increased productivity).

d. THE WARNING SIGNS

How do you know when stress is getting to your workforce?

There are many danger signs, including lack of interest and enthusiasm, low morale, high turnover, absenteeism, tension, low productivity, high number of accidents, lack of cooperation, impulsive decision making, negative attitude or cynicism, disregard for high priority tasks, inappropriate humor, poor interpersonal relationships, high anxiety, depression, and boredom.

The benefits to the employer of recognizing and taking steps to deal with the effects of stress are many and include —

(a) higher employee morale,

(b) enhanced team spirit,

(c) improved decision making,

(d) decreases in absenteeism and turnover, and

(e) decreases in insurance expenses/medical costs.

Productivity and motivation are becoming major concerns for employers throughout the country. Both job stress and job burnout take a physical and emotional toll on the workforce. Therefore, more and more employers are trying to fight the problem *before* it becomes a problem. One way they are doing this is to introduce wellness programs.

e. THE BENEFITS OF WELLNESS/HEALTH PROGRAMS

Stress has been called the "black lung" of the technical class. Fortunately, employers are beginning to understand the connection between mental performance and physical fitness. There are many indications that employee wellness programs really do decrease absenteeism and may also increase productivity.

Many firms have started wellness programs. These programs offer employees a positive way to stay healthy and help resolve problems that might interfere with work.

Heart disease, cancer, and accidents are the leading causes of death for people under 65. These same problems drag down a company's productivity. Fortunately, more and more companies are finding that these health problems can be curbed by eliminating smoking, ensuring proper exercise and diet, and controlling high blood pressure.

In addition to combating physical problems, wellness plans also respond to other employees' interests. Often this results in improved morale and greater employee loyalty to the company.

In Sweden, it has been official policy for nearly 30 years to move non-active workers into more active roles. Studies in Sweden have shown that industrial exercise programs lead to fewer sick days and fewer hospital admissions.

Dr. Roy J. Shephard, professor of preventive medicine and director of the University of Toronto School of Physical and Health Education, conducted a study of the home office staffs of two insurance companies in Toronto. He used the

North American Life Assurance Co. as his control group for comparison with the Canada Life Assurance Co.

The Canada Life people met 3 times weekly for 30-minute sessions to do exercises that included rhythmic calisthenics, jogging, and games to increase endurance and cardiovascular fitness. They met for six months. Among the employees who worked out at least twice a week, turnover dropped from 15% to 1.5% and absenteeism fell 22%. The majority of those who exercised regularly realized "substantial gains in conventional measures of fitness, such as body fat, aerobic power, and flexibility."

Tenneco, a large energy-related company in Houston, has also had great success with its health and fitness program. Tenneco's health and fitness program initially had six main objectives:

(a) To increase the level of employees' cardiovascular fitness

(b) To increase employees' knowledge of positive health habits and reduce coronary risk factors

(c) To obtain employee ownership in the program and promote self-responsibility

(d) To motivate employees to improve and/or maintain their optimum standards of health

(e) To further develop the above objectives with interested Tenneco divisions outside the Houston area

(f) To further develop program adherence by involving the employees' support groups (families, friends, and peers)

Tenneco's program was chosen as the top corporate program in 1984 by both the Washington Business Group on Health and the Association for Fitness in Business.

Scherer Brothers Lumber Co. of Minneapolis has had a company wellness program in effect since fall of 1980. First, printed health information was distributed over a four-week period followed by questionnaires. The questionnaires were designed to provide each employee with a "lifestyle profile" indicating which of them would benefit from health seminars on specific topics. Seminars on nutrition, exercise, stress management, smoking, and self-care motivation were made available.

The company replaced office candy-vending machines with fruit juice machines. They removed cigarette machines. They filled the coffee machines with decaffeinated coffee. They also provided free popcorn and fruit for snacks.

According to Greg Scherer, co-owner of the company, the wellness program resulted in lower health insurance premiums and workers' compensation claims and increased productivity. Scherer Lumber's absenteeism rate is 0.3%. This compares with 3% for the industry.

f. THE STEPS TO AN EFFECTIVE PROGRAM

1. Involve top management

In order for wellness programs to work effectively, top management must be involved and supportive. A company must commit adequate money and staff to meet the goals of the program. Company leaders should visibly support the program through their own participation.

2. Designate responsibility

Designate someone to be responsible for the program. It's important that responsibility is centered in one area and coordinated by one person. That person is very often the personnel administrator.

Often, a company will establish a committee to look into the need for establishing a wellness program. The person who is responsible for the program should also approve the establishment of a planning committee. Committee members may include representatives from personnel, medical claims, the medical department, marketing, union affairs, and line employees. Through the committee, the company is able to determine the needs and interests of employees, develop a plan, recruit program participants, and implement and evaluate the program.

3. Determine the need

Conduct a survey to determine employee interest. This survey can be prepared very simply by the planning committee and distributed through inter-office mail. You're looking for two things: an indication of the *level* of interest in employer-sponsored "wellness," and an indication of the *areas* of interest among employees. For example, your particular employee group might not be interested in a quit-smoking program (maybe very few employees smoke), but they would be interested in company-sponsored aerobics. You won't know unless you give them the opportunity to tell you.

In determining what type of services to provide, a brief questionnaire is often distributed to employees. Some companies use specially designed forms called "health risk appraisals." These forms are computer analyzed and provide in-depth health information to both employees and management.

4. Identify resources

Determine company and community resources. Many communities have access to health maintenance organizations (HMOs) — an increasingly popular form of health care where a group of doctors gets together to provide services through insurance programs sponsored by companies. These HMOs are actively sponsoring various health-related programs for the community. In addition, many health organizations (such as the American Heart Association) work with corporations to promote healthy lifestyles. Your first step is to determine what type of support is already available in your community. Then, you need to present this information to management and ask for some commitment of funds, space, time, etc., for developing a program. It's important that you know what your resources are before you begin planning.

When identifying available resources, a company needs to consider existing health services (including health screening), existing facilities (including community services), the skills and talents of employees, available community options such as free information about wellness, fee-for-service providers, and consultants experienced in the design, implementation, and evaluation of such programs.

Not large enough to fund a full-scale health-care program? Many companies aren't — but there are still ways to provide wellness benefits to employees. A company on a very small budget needs only to provide room to move around and a place to change clothes. Fancy exercise equipment is not essential. However, good training people are essential. One of the most common options chosen by companies that cannot accommodate a program on their premises is the company-paid or partially paid membership in a local health club or YMCA.

5. Establish objectives

As with any endeavor, it's important to have specific goals to work toward as a group. These goals could be something like a certain percentage of all employees participating in the program, or specific health-maintenance concerns such as pounds lost, blood pressure decrease, decrease in smoking employees, etc. Your goals should be jointly established by employees and the committee and progress toward these goals should be communicated on a regular basis. You should choose goals that can be monitored to evaluate the program.

You should also assist employees in setting realistic personal goals. Offer incentives for such things as quitting smoking, lowered blood pressure, weight loss, etc. The employee sets the goal and develops his or her own individual program, but the employer participates by encouraging the employee in his or her endeavors and offering various perks (time off, gift certificates, etc.) for reaching pre-established goals.

6. Conduct individual health assessments

Each employee who chooses to participate in the program should be assessed before the onset of the program. Whether you do this on-site (through a company nurse, etc.) or through outside providers, it's important that employees get a "clean bill of health" before they embark on any form of health program.

7. Monitor effectiveness

Finally, you will want to be able to monitor the effectiveness of the program itself. You'll need to consider employee participation, drop-out rates, and changes in employee health knowledge, attitudes, and behavior. You'll also want to look at long-term effectiveness in terms of decreased absenteeism, use of health-care benefits, number of accidents, and increases in productivity.

13
TAKING CARE OF THE KIDS

It used to be that someone was home during the day — someone to watch the children, run the errands, cook the meals, clean the house. That someone has traditionally been the woman. Now, having someone at home to take care of these important duties is more the exception than the rule.

The Employee Benefit Research Institute has predicted that childcare will become the "fringe benefit of the 1990s." And well it should. The labor force now includes 70% of all women with children between the ages of 6 and 17 and more than half of the women with children less than 1 year old.

These changes are having a dramatic impact on your work force. According to the National Association of Bank Women, today's businesses face five critical challenges:

1. The impending labor shortage

2. The need for women to fill two of three new jobs

3. The decline in productivity growth that threatens competitiveness

4. The demand for a more educated work force

5. The shift from manufacturing to service jobs

Employers need to be prepared to deal with the childcare issue in order to meet these challenges. Why? Because the shift in societal roles affects your work force in two very important ways. Employees are affected, first, by increased stress caused by the increased responsibility of trying to hold down a full-time job and manage the home concurrently and second, by concern over the shortage of quality dependent care coupled with feelings of guilt over not spending enough time with the family.

These strong feelings lead to stress which leads to lack of productivity. As an employer, you hold a key role in reducing these feelings of stress.

What role does the business world play in the two-career dilemma? As more and more families are choosing both two careers *and* children, an increasingly larger one. This dilemma also presents an opportunity to some employers. Companies can gain a competitive edge by offering corporate childcare. Corporate childcare is one of the new perks of the nineties.

Aside from the pure altruism of wanting to respond to employees' needs in this area, companies are feeling compelled to be responsive due to a shrinking work force and the need to compete for the best workers by offering progressive family policies — for both female and male employees. It's important to note that studies at DuPont found that men's reports of family-related problems nearly doubled during the period of 1985 to 1988. Keep in mind as well that dependent care does not only involve children. Studies done at Travelers Insurance Company and IBM have shown that 20% to 30% of all employees had some responsibility for the care of an adult dependent.

a. UNDERSTANDING THE ISSUES

Today's two-career marriages often involve more than two people. Many involve children or other dependents — a complicating factor that can cause as much frustration for an employer as it can for parents.

For employers, concern often involves:

(a) When will a new mother (or father) return to work?

(b) How much time will be lost on the job due to dependent care problems?

(c) What effect will worrying about a young or ailing family member have on productivity?

(d) How will other workers react to the special requirements of working parents and caregivers?

For employees, concern involves:

(a) How much time will I be able to spend at home with the new child?

(b) Where will I find qualified dependent care?*

(c) What do I do when dependents are sick?

(d) Will the boss be flexible in terms of hours worked?

(e) What effect will part-time parenting have on the children?

A survey conducted by the National Association of Bank Women (NABW) reported that 74% of the respondents had no employer-provided childcare benefits. The survey further revealed that working parents spend as much as 12.5% of their work week dealing with some aspect of childcare.

Companies are finding that they must begin to respond to these needs. And they are.

There are three important areas where employers are in a position to provide support and assistance to employees concerned about caring for their families: parental leave policies, flexible scheduling or understanding the "3:00 syndrome," and the establishment of company-subsidized or company-sponsored childcare. We'll take a look at each.

---

*Because the care of children is the more common type of dependent care, this chapter will focus on that area. However, the same principles do, in most cases, also apply to care of other dependents such as elderly parents.

b. PARENTAL LEAVE POLICIES

Maternity leave is a common option offered to a company's expectant parents. In the U.S., the 1978 Pregnancy Discrimination Act requires companies to treat pregnancy as any other disability and offer paid disability leave to female employees. Consequently, most employees return to work after the allowed six to eight weeks of paid leave. Among higher income women, two out of three return within four months, according to a 1983 study.

However, the United States continues to lag behind some more progressive countries. A Columbia University study reports that every Western industrial nation except the United States mandates some form of maternity leave.

Catalyst, a national, nonprofit organization promoting the career advancement of women in business, conducted a comprehensive national survey of the top 1,000 industrial companies and 500 other companies. They included financial as well as other service companies in this study. In the initial phase, their key findings were as follows:

(a) Of the companies studied, 95% offer disability benefits. Very few (7.4%), however, offer paid leave above and beyond the disability benefits. More than one-half (51.7%) offer unpaid leaves to females.

(b) More and more companies are offering leaves for men. In an earlier Catalyst survey, only 8.6% of the companies surveyed offered paternity benefits. In this recent survey, more than one-third gave males some unpaid leave time.

(c) Men and women are often offered comparable unpaid leaves, although men seldom take advantage of them. When men do accept unpaid paternity leaves, they usually return to the workplace sooner than they have to.

According to another survey, more than one-third of all companies have unpaid leave for men. Most of them offer packages similar to those they offer women employees. Yet fewer men take their employers up on the offer. This may be because many companies do little to publicize these programs and/or because there are still negative stereotypes against men who take time off to help raise children.

Many companies are increasing the involvement of expectant mothers in planning for their absence. Women can decide which employees should be assigned to various duties. They can provide specific guidelines for special projects. Thus, the fear of being forgotten or easily replaced is reduced.

Another option offered by more and more companies is working at home. Women can arrange to work on special projects at home while they are on leave. Again, women feel more needed because of the availability of this option.

c. THE 3:00 SYNDROME AND WHAT YOU CAN (AND SHOULD!) DO ABOUT IT

A new term has entered our vocabulary: the "three o'clock syndrome." It refers to reduced productivity and higher error and accident rates as employees begin thinking of their children around the time school gets out. This drop in productivity, however, can occur at any time. Let's take a look at a few examples.

Sam's son started kindergarten last week. Sam has been noticeably preoccupied at work and has been spending an inordinate amount of time on the phone. He needs to come in later so he can see his son off to school and needs to leave earlier so he can be there when the bus drops him off.

Joelle's preteen son is having problems in school. She receives numerous calls from the principal each week and is often asked to come to the school.

Jerry's daughter is in preschool, but frequently ill. He often needs to take days off work to care for her, even though he and his wife "take turns" with this particular responsibility.

Illness, non-standard work schedules, teacher's conferences, school plays — these are just a few of the special circumstances that working parents find themselves involved in. Most parents hesitate to bring up their personal concerns in the work setting. They struggle through these upsets, trying their hardest to focus on their jobs. They often fail.

It is simply not possible to separate one's personal from one's professional life. The two are inextricably intermeshed; what happens in one area can't help but affect the other.

As employers, the first step you can take to alleviate some of these difficulties is to be concerned. Understanding and allowing for flexible scheduling is one of the simplest and most appreciated steps you can take.

Very often it is just not possible for a working parent to maintain the hours of 8:00 a.m. to 5:00 p.m. without frequent adjustments. Children get sick. They have doctor's appointments, they have days off school, and so on. Letting your employees know that you're aware of these needs, and taking steps to communicate a flexible policy to managers (so they can, in turn, pass this information to employees) will go a long way towards alleviating the stress of trying to balance responsibilities to children with responsibilities to the job.

Flextime, part-time work, and job sharing are arrangements many U.S. companies are introducing to reduce workers' childcare pressures. Approximately one-third of the Fortune 1300 companies offer their employees personal or sick child leave when family members are ill. Flexplace is another option which allows employees to work at home for a specified number of hours per work week.

Emery Apparel Canada Inc. of Edmonton has a four-day work week because most of its 200 employees are married women. Emery also offers free expert lectures on such issues as raising teenagers.

d. THE DAYCARE DILEMMA

A primary concern for employees is finding quality care for the children. Today, two-paycheck families have become the rule rather than the exception. Suddenly the question is not "Should we send our child to a daycare center?" but "How do we choose the best place?"

It may be encouraging to many of your employees to know most experts agree that daycare has several advantages for children. For example, it gives children independence and the chance to form individual identities at an early age. Studies have shown that children who have attended daycare centers before beginning school learn to read sooner than those who have not had this advantage. They are also able to develop other academic skills more quickly. Children are better able to talk to others since they're comfortable with both adults and other children, and they establish a better idea of individual sex roles. This is particularly important in single parent households.

Is there a benefit to be gained by companies that provide special services to working parents? Studies and experiences of companies that do offer these services indicate there is. A growing body of evidence shows that company-sponsored daycare pays off in terms of both increased productivity and better morale.

Helping employees with childcare can reduce the stress workers feel. A 1985 study of 650 employees in a large, Boston-based corporation reported that balancing work and family responsibilities is the heaviest contributor to depression among employees — male and female.

187

Companies have also found that absenteeism and turn-over can be reduced. After establishing the Northside Child Development Center in Minneapolis, Control Data Corporation studied 90 employees over a 20-month period. Thirty mothers with children in Northside were matched with a sample of 30 mothers using other childcare arrangements and 30 employees with no children or grown children. The average monthly absenteeism rate for daycare users in the company-sponsored center was 4.4%. This compared with 6.02% for non-participants in the two control groups. The average monthly turnover rate among program users was 1.77%. This compared with 6.3% for nonparticipants.

Now, as more and more employers are dealing with childcare worries, they are asking themselves, "What can we do to keep these workers, and keep them happy?" Some are already exploring the various options.

Hoffmann-La Roche began sponsoring childcare services for employees in 1977. Today it operates a subsidized center a block from its headquarters. At the National Governors Association Conference on Day Care in 1985, Leonard Silverman, vice president of human resources at Hoffmann-La Roche said, "We consider support for childcare to be an investment — one that has already paid us handsome dividends."

Nyloncraft, an Indiana plastic molding manufacturer, had concerns about worker absenteeism. Turnover was at a record high. Anxious to find out why, the company asked its employees. They found that the problem was finding convenient and affordable childcare. Their solution was to open Nyloncraft Learning Center (NLC). Open 24 hours a day (to accommodate the night shift) and run by a 27-person staff, NLC offers the best in childcare. Worker absenteeism and turnover have never been lower.

What can you do? There are three primary areas of employee childcare assistance: on- or near-site childcare centers, childcare vouchers and financial assistance, and information and referral services.

1. On-site or near-site childcare centers

With this option, an employer (like Hoffmann-La Roche) operates a childcare facility on company premises or provides support to a nearby center.

Employers choose to either run the program themselves or rent space to a professional organization. Employees may pay for the program according to a sliding-fee scale. Kinder-Care, the largest for-profit daycare chain in the U.S., runs several programs. Their services are provided to companies such as Campbell Soup Company and Disney World.

Companies can also help organize family daycare providers, neighborhood people who care for up to six children in their homes. Many parents prefer this home-like setting for very young children. Several companies have hired local agencies to recruit, train, and license family daycare providers along their employees' commuting paths.

In addition to focusing on the everyday childcare needs of employees, some companies have developed ways to deal with absenteeism associated with sick children. Hewlett-Packard and Levi Strauss have jointly established a 15-bed infirmary attached to a daycare center in San Jose, California. The 3M Company in Minnesota pays 70% of the charges for in-home nursing services offered by Children's Hospital in St. Paul when children are sick.

2. Childcare vouchers and financial assistance

About 500 businesses offer vouchers to their workers, according to one employee benefits specialist. With this type of system, a company pays care providers directly to secure a reduced rate for its employees.

Several follow a standard format like the one worked out with Kinder-Care Learning Centers. A 10% discount to industry participants is given if the employer provides a matching amount. This results in a 20% price reduction for the employee.

Other companies use flexible benefit programs (see chapter 10 for a detailed discussion). These programs let employees choose from a variety of benefits. Flexible benefit programs are usually cheaper for employers than vouchers. About 2,000 employers now provide flexible benefits, and approximately 50% to 75% of their plans offer dependent care as an option.

The voucher system gives employees coupons worth money toward the cost of childcare services. The coupons purchase licensed childcare and allow parents to make all the decisions about childcare arrangements.

Polaroid Corporation covers a portion of the childcare costs for employees whose yearly family incomes are under $25,000. The Measurex Corporation pays $100 per month for childcare costs during an infant's first year. Baxter Travenol Laboratories in Illinois and Palmetto (Florida) Hospital confine vouchers to a selected group of daycare centers. Zayre Corporation reimburses employees $20 a week for any childcare they choose for their children five years old and under.

3. Information and referral

With an information and referral (I & R) system, the company offers information about childcare services to employees free of charge. Some companies contract with local information and referral agencies that maintain computerized lists of available childcare services. An I & R agency researches local facilities and publishes its findings regularly for the company's staff. Details on location, age groups, hours, and number of openings available are provided.

About 900 companies offer I & R to their employees, either directly or through specialized agencies. Steelcase Inc. offers employee access to two childcare specialists who conduct parenting workshops. They also help workers find appropriate community resources. Other companies provide employee seminars during the workday.

A study conducted by the National Employer Supported Child Care Project reports that the number of companies offering childcare programs increased nearly 400% from 1978 to 1982. About 2,500 companies offer some form of childcare assistance.

For other companies, childcare benefits may become more a requirement of doing business than a luxury.

In one of his books, Lee Iaccoca makes the point that he has never yet heard a retired worker lament that "I wish I had spent more time at the office." Today's employees are making the decision well before retirement that their families come first.

To maintain a motivated work force, to compete in the labor market, to assure themselves of a successful future, employers must be cognizant of this shift in attitude and take a proactive approach to meeting their employees' changing needs.

14
EDUCATION AND TRAINING:
A TWO-WAY BENEFIT

Higher education and business are basically interdependent. One needs money to produce educated people, and the other needs educated people to produce money. — Milton Eisenhower

a. A HISTORICAL PERSPECTIVE

Education and training for employees is not new. In fact, the first program for employee education began in the late 19th century. It was started by the National Cash Register Co. (NCR). In 1894, John H. Patterson, the founder of NCR, set up a school for salesmen at his company's Dayton, Ohio, headquarters. Employees were taught to deliver a proven sales pitch. In 1903, in what may have been the first management training program in the country, Patterson set up a school for top-performing salesmen near Dayton.

In 1926, General Motors Corp. took the step of buying two private management schools. These schools were renamed General Motors Institute. Higher-level management skills such as finance and marketing were taught to supervisors and engineers.

In 1928, Harvard University established the first university program for working managers. That summer, 170 executives spent six weeks studying a condensed version of Harvard's MBA program.

b. CURRENT TRENDS

There is a growing trend toward continuing education training — that is, training that is in addition to the education employees may have received in college. Every year, approximately 5,000,000 people attend a continuing education program.

Many factors have caused an increased demand for continuing education — from both corporations and individuals. One of the most important is the increased competition for available jobs. This is due to the "baby boom," a greater number of women in the job market, and more and more workers staying on the job past retirement age. Other factors are rapid technological change — especially in the computer and medical fields — and the rising educational level of the population.

According to a recent Carnegie Foundation report, corporations spend at least $40 billion per year on employee training and development. Prior to their breakup, Bell Telephone was spending a billion dollars each year on training. It's expected that businesses will be even more involved in executive education than they have in the past.

Today, countless organizations across the country are finding that education is yet another way to motivate their workers. Courses can be offered to employees at virtually every level of the organization. At Tassani Communications Inc., a Chicago advertising agency, for example, employees can attend "Food for Thought" brown-bag lunches and listen to lectures on topics ranging from stress management to crime prevention to time management. CEO Sally Tassani says that the lunches are "an inexpensive way to make this a fun place to work and learn." Universities have been created by Dana Corp., Walt Disney Productions, and McDonald's. IBM currently spends approximately $500 million annually on employee training and education. AT&T has extensive executive-education programs for middle and top managers with courses that include management training, congressional staff assignments, and executive exchanges with government agencies. Employees at Gulf Oil, IBM, GE, Xerox, TRW, and GM all have access to career-planning programs to help them select life goals and accomplish career objectives. More than 9,000 managers and professionals have used the service at GE.

Tektronix, Inc., an electronics firm in Beaverton, Oregon, uses education to attract, retain, and develop people. The company offers seven different degree programs, as well as supplemental and specific skill courses in off- and on-site programs. These programs are reimbursed up to 100%. Employees often go on flexible schedules to attend courses. Employee development is also promoted by Tektronix through job posting, internal promotion, career workshops, career counseling, flextime, and childcare. They also have a handbook that describes job opportunities and the educational requirements and salaries of specific positions.

In *Training Magazine's* 1984 organizational survey, nearly 90% of the respondents offered some form of formal training in management skills and development. Asked to estimate the number of hours of formal training the typical employee in several specific job categories would receive, respondents answered:

Executives	28.3
Senior Managers	22.7
Middle Managers	32.5
First-line Sups/Foremen	32.5
Sales Reps	19.5
Professionals	27.2
Administrative Employees	11.9
Office/Secretarial	10.8

| Production Workers | 12.3 |
| Customer Service Employees | 13.4 |

According to Peter Drucker, "The productivity of knowledge has already become the key to productivity, competitive strength and economic achievement. Knowledge has already become the primary industry, the industry that supplies the economy with the essential and central resources of production."

c. THE BENEFITS OF EMPLOYEE EDUCATION

Employee education offers many benefits. The benefits include improved attitudes, increased knowledge and skill, higher productivity, improved profitability, better employee morale, and improved company image.Benefits to individual employees include increased knowledge, better attitude, and improved performance. Employees can also achieve promotions, personal growth, and a sense of satisfaction.

Training sessions can be enjoyable and productive — or they can be boring and a waste of time. Whether you're training your employees through in-house programs or attendance at public seminars, you want to make sure that they're getting the best training possible.

If you're considering the establishment of a training plan, there are two options to look at: in-house or outside services.

d. IN-HOUSE TRAINING

There are several types of in-house training ranging from supervisory coaching of employees to actual training seminars. Other options include informal discussion groups and self-development through computer-assisted instruction or videotape. The personnel or training department plays a major role in any of these areas. Our focus here will be on in-house seminars.

195

For any in-house training program to work effectively, it's important to have top management support. To get this support, the training personnel need to demonstrate a need for training, do a good job of developing trial programs, and show proof of a positive result.

The two major objections will be that training "costs too much" and "we're too busy to worry about this now." The response to both these objections can be, "We can't afford *not* to worry about it now."

Once support is achieved and you're on your way to a formal training effort, the following factors are important:

(a) A central authority must carry out and monitor the training process.

(b) The role of the central authority should be clearly defined.

(c) Managers and supervisors must participate from the beginning. They will need to be convinced of the need for training. They will also need to understand the important role they have in the success of this training.

(d) An information campaign should be instituted. Employees must know about the training opportunities the company is offering. Training needs to be promoted as a positive aspect of employment.

(e) Initial training efforts should be aimed at areas that are ripe for training.

(f) Supervisors should be encouraged to talk about courses with subordinates before training starts.

(g) Employees going through the training should complete end-of-course action plans to help use the techniques and skills learned.

(h) Follow-up training must be provided to help the learning process and encourage retention.

(i) Managers and supervisors should aid in the design of training.

(j) Employee response to the training must be continually monitored.

The major advantage of having in-house training is the time allowed for the development of training programs that are specific to employee needs. In addition, there is the opportunity to monitor training results on an on-going basis. Training offerings can be changed as necessary.

If, however, your company is too small or management simply will not support the development of in-house training, there is another option you can explore. You can look into public seminars.

e. CHOOSING OUTSIDE TRAINING

An article in the *Wall Street Journal* once stated "people who go to seminars these days sometimes learn more than anything else the importance of picking seminars carefully."

There are several things to look for (and look out for) when examining public seminar offerings.

1. The topic

When an employee comes to you with a brochure on a seminar there's no doubt that the first thing you look for is the topic. Is it something that would benefit the company? Is it related to the job being done? Will it provide the information needed? These are just a few of the questions you ask as you look at the title and outline. For many businesspeople the topic is one of the most important factors in their decision of whether to send an employee to a program.

2. Speakers

No matter how well the topic fits your needs, you won't want to send an employee to a seminar unless you can be sure that the speakers have something worthwhile to offer. Have you heard of the people speaking at the program? What is their reputation? What comments have you heard about them from others?

3. Sponsor

A flashy brochure doesn't guarantee a quality presentation. If you're not familiar with the sponsor of a program you've heard about, you should try to gather some information before signing anyone up for the program. Call and request names of prior attendees you can use for references. Ask around. Has anyone you know attended any program sponsored by this organization? What was their impression?

4. Level of the program

The level of the program will affect your overall impression. Even if someone has been in a particular field for several years, they may need to attend a basic program introducing an innovation or technical change. If an employee is new to a job, but has very high technical knowledge, an "intermediate" program may be what you're looking for.

5. Handout materials

Only a certain amount of learning can take place in a lecture situation. Many seminar attendees prefer seminars that provide high quality written materials they will be able to use as a reference after the program.

6. Format

What will be the style of presentation? Will it be a lecture format? Workshop? One-on-one? Will there be one speaker? A panel? A series of short lectures? Format considerations vary with individual preference and, of course, the topic of discussion. With each seminar you consider you should ask, "Is this the best format for getting the information?"

7. Time/cost

The cost of a program goes beyond the price in the brochure. It also includes the price of travel and accommodations and the price of an employee's time away from the office.

8. Location

Location is also a consideration. An attractive location is an added incentive for employees. If quality is lacking, however, the company may not be getting much value from the employee's experience.

f. SUMMARY

Does continuing education lead to greater professional competence? The growing number of people attending (and re-attending) these programs would seem to indicate that it does.

Keep in mind, however, the warning, "let the buyer beware." Choose carefully to be sure that you and your company are spending your education dollars wisely.

When choosing programming, whether it's developed in-house or offered by an outside organization, you need to do the following:

(a) Review potential benefits

(b) Review available programs

(c) Select participants carefully

(d) Plan ahead

(e) Counsel with the participant before the program

(f) Discuss the program with the participant after the program

(g) Help the participant plan for future development

15
CONCLUSION

Money *isn't* everything. Cold, hard cash isn't the answer to problems with poor morale, low productivity, high absenteeism, or bad attitudes. Today's employees require much, much more. They require *commitment.* They require *loyalty.* They require *involvement.* They require all of the things we've covered and they require these things on a consistent basis.

Certainly instituting wellness programs, offering educational opportunities, or developing recognition programs means a cost to your company: monetary cost. And the investment of your *time* in providing employees with the feedback and nurturing they need to do a good job is, in its purest form, an investment of money because your time is your company's money.

However, if you *don't* offer these things to your existing employees, it's going to cost you far more in the long run — in recruitment of replacement employees, in training, and in turnover.

Let's take a look at what happened to one company (which will remain nameless) that attempted to respond to low productivity by "cleaning house." They hired a management consultant (a.k.a. hatchet man) to do the dirty job of getting rid of "dead wood." This man's tactics included forbidding employees to keep personal items in their work areas, on their walls, or on their desks. Gone were the photos of family, the posters, and the plants that had enabled employees to call their work spaces "home." He developed a hardline approach to time off. He implemented split shifts ınd required overtime, even where workloads had not necessitated such tactics in the past. And he told employees that if they didn't like it they could find another job.

Did productivity increase? Yes, initially. But fear rarely works as a motivator for extended periods of time and eventually turnover rates increased dramatically. However, it wasn't the ineffective employees who decided to seek employment elsewhere. The valued employees, worried about their job security, went job hunting and of course they were successful. The cost to the company was substantial. Hiring and training became a way of life. Nobody *volunteered* to work extra time any more. Employees had no assurance that their company was committed or loyal to them and so they were no longer committed or loyal to their company.

Any number of platitudes apply as well in a business setting as in other walks of life. "Do unto others as you would have them do unto you"… "You reap what you sow"… "One good deed deserves another." Nonmonetary incentives are nothing more than the business world's opportunity to put these platitudes into practice. The companies that do this, and do it well, quickly find that any costs they incur are outpaced by the benefits they gain from their loyal, motivated employees. In fact, time after time, these companies find that they reap *more* than they've sown. So can you.